Eva K. Bowlby P
311 North W
Waynesburg, PA 1

P9-ARK-894

How the
Inner Master Works

*This book
donated in loving
memory of*

Gladys B. Kettering

Also by Harold Klemp

Ask the Master, Book 1
Ask the Master, Book 2
Child in the Wilderness
The Living Word
Soul Travelers of the Far Country
The Spiritual Exercises of ECK
The Temple of ECK
The Wind of Change

The Mahanta Transcripts Series

Journey of Soul, Book 1
How to Find God, Book 2
The Secret Teachings, Book 3
The Golden Heart, Book 4
Cloak of Consciousness, Book 5
Unlocking the Puzzle Box, Book 6
The Eternal Dreamer, Book 7
The Dream Master, Book 8
We Come as Eagles, Book 9
The Drumbeat of Time, Book 10
What Is Spiritual Freedom? Book 11

Stories to Help You See
God in Your Life

The Book of ECK Parables, Volume 1
The Book of ECK Parables, Volume 2
The Book of ECK Parables, Volume 3
The Book of ECK Parables, Volume 4

MAHANTA

This book has been authored by and published under the supervision of the Mahanta, the Living ECK Master, Sri Harold Klemp. It is the Word of ECK.

How the
Inner Master Works

Harold Klemp

Mahanta Transcripts
Book 12

ECKANKAR
Minneapolis, MN

,

How the Inner Master Works
Mahanta Transcripts, Book 12

Copyright © 1995 ECKANKAR

All rights reserved. No part of this book may be reproduced, stored in a retrieval system, or transmitted in any form by any means, whether electronic, mechanical, photocopying, recording, or otherwise, without prior written permission of ECKANKAR.

The terms ECKANKAR, ECK, EK, MAHANTA, SOUL TRAVEL, and VAIRAGI, among others, are trademarks of ECKANKAR, P.O. Box 27300, Minneapolis, MN 55427 U.S.A.

Printed in U.S.A.

Compiled by Joan Klemp and Anne Pezdirc
Edited by Anthony Moore and Mary Carroll Moore

Cover design by Lois Stanfield
Cover illustration by Joann Ballinger
Text illustrations by Valerie Taglieri and Ron Wennekes
Text photo (page xii) by Sandro Pasetto
Back cover photo by Robert Huntley

Library of Congress Cataloging-in-Publication Data

Klemp, Harold.
    How the inner master works / Harold Klemp.
        p. cm. — (Mahanta transcripts ; bk.12)
    Includes index.
    ISBN 1-57043-103-5 (alk. paper)
    1. Eckankar (Organization) 2. Spiritual life. 3. Dreams—
Religious aspects. I. Title. II. Series: Klemp, Harold. Mahanta
transcripts ; bk. 12.
BP605.E3K5567 1995
299'.93—dc20   95-30093
                                                         CIP

Contents

Withdrawn

Life's Movement • Inner Master • One Cup of Coffee •
Dream Help for Everyday Life • Tighten the Belt • The
Dream World Is Real • Lessons on Earth • Path of Truth
• Dream Meeting before ECK • Singing HU to Yourself
• An Ancient Blessing

Foreword

The Way of the Eternal, *The Shariyat-Ki-Sugmad,* Book One, states: "The knowledge that the true, living Master gives is direct and immediate, coming from actual Soul experiences apart from the physical senses and human consciousness. His words are charged with the ECK currents surging within him. They sink into the inner self of the listener, leaving little doubt about the existence of Soul experiences."

Sri Harold Klemp, the Mahanta, the Living ECK Master travels in all parts of the world to give the sacred teachings of ECK. Many of his public talks have been released on video- and audiocassette, but others have never before been available beyond the particular seminar at which he spoke.

As a special service to the students of ECK and truth seekers everywhere, all of Sri Harold's public talks are being transcribed and edited under his direction. Now these transcripts can be study aids for your greater spiritual understanding.

How the Inner Master Works, Mahanta Transcripts, Book 12, contains his talks from 1992–93. May they serve to uplift you to a greater vision of life.

Sri Harold Klemp, the Mahanta, the Living ECK Master tells how to get answers from God in our dreams, every-day coincidences, and daily spiritual exercises.

1

Graceful Living

A Year of Graceful Living is the theme for this new spiritual year in ECK.

Graceful living, being gracious, means that you are filled with the blessings of God. And if you are filled with the blessings of God, you will certainly be someone who lives gracefully and graciously with others.

Key of Opportunity

I was in the post office about two weeks ago when a father came in with his very small daughter. She started to run back and forth in the lobby, clutching a key.

When I went over to my box to get my mail, the little girl followed me and watched as I put the key in the lock and unlocked it. She seemed fascinated by the process. Apparently she had tried her key in several of the boxes, and it hadn't opened any of them.

She stood there and watched as I locked my mailbox. By then her father had completed his business and was ready to go.

Scooping up his little girl, he started out the door, then turned back to me and said, "When you're that age and you've got a key, the whole world is a lock."

I thought about what he had said, trying to unlock the spiritual message. For a child, the whole world is an opportunity, a mystery, something to unlock and see what's in there. Will this work?

Will the key work?

Forest Family

Now a quick update on the animals and birds at home in Minnesota.

We started out with sparrows five years ago, right after I bought little bird feeders, placed them in the yard on poles, and put some seed in them. At the time I wondered if it was the right kind of seed and if any birds would actually come.

That afternoon a few sparrows found the bird feeders and seemed to enjoy themselves. I felt so needed, so happy. Then came the blackbirds, pretty soon the blue jays, and even a goldfinch.

Eventually I got rid of the little bird feeders on poles; they were too much trouble in the winter. I put some dishes on the ground, and pretty soon we had raccoons, squirrels, rabbits, and chipmunks. Lately we've even had visits from deer. And this is in the city.

Learning Bravery

Some say the rabbit is a symbol of fear. Maybe that's why our rabbit, Stretch, is so cautious when he comes up to the feeding dish, day or night.

His only defense is his speed, so you might say his fear is what keeps him alive. He has grown into a big old rabbit.

Just the other day a beautiful six-point buck and a doe showed up at the feeding dishes. I heard a loud noise in the little forest—actually it's brush—outside our window, and looked out to see the buck bumping the doe out of the way. He wanted all the food for himself.

The deer is one of the symbols for gentleness, and that huge buck was not living up to his character. But the rabbit sat at the dish opposite the buck, about four or five feet away. I was so proud of Stretch. He didn't back off at all.

The buck hadn't learned anything about gentleness, but the rabbit was learning something about bravery.

And so the little community in our backyard changes. The animals and birds that come and go are part of our family. Sometimes they fight with each other over the food—sparrows with other sparrows, cardinals with other cardinals, and so on—yet they are a family. In their own way they get along.

A Spiritual Community

Each of the little families makes up a spiritual community.

They are all learning lessons about when to come to the feed dish, and they all have their scheduled times. The rabbit and squirrels are about equal. If the rabbit comes and finds the squirrels are already there, he waits. If the rabbit is there first, the squirrels get a little pushy and boisterous, but they wait until the rabbit decides to leave the dish.

The chipmunk, though just a little bitty guy, has as much nerve as I've seen but no grace at all. He'll come out of the woods, so short he can hardly see over the grass—at least not the way I cut it, which isn't often.

You can actually see his trail into the brush because his belly is so close to the ground.

But small or not, he'll see the squirrels gathered around one of the dishes, come up behind them, and zip right through their group.

He scares the living daylights out of them and sends them scurrying up the trees. Then he makes one more swing through the turtledoves, who go flying up in the air. Pretty soon this tiny chipmunk, probably the smallest of the creatures out there, has the dish all to himself.

He doesn't have a lot of grace, but he does get the dish.

I've noticed too that the squirrels outrank the blue jays. If four or five squirrels have the dish, the blue jays have to wait. But they're smart — and loud.

They'll start screeching and shrieking the way birds do, with their little screams of, "Danger! Danger!" When the squirrels run off into the trees, the blue jays come down and take over the dish.

Our backyard community is a very clever little family.

How We Treat Each Other

Often I watch them and think how much they are like people. People also divide themselves in one way or another—whether by age, race, religion, political affiliation, or some other category. At the same time they forget that we are all God's creatures.

In ECK our name for God is SUGMAD, but the name doesn't change a thing. What really matters is how people treat each other in the human community.

A television program about dolphins called them the second most intelligent mammals on earth. I asked my wife, "Well, who's the first?"

4

Accept What You Have Now

An initiate who has been in ECK for a number of years said to me today, "You've written other, more advanced discourses. When will we get to see them?" Several initiates have asked the same question.

In the first year that someone becomes a member of ECKANKAR, I send them a discourse series they can study to learn the basic spiritual principles of the Light and Sound of God. Since I write new discourses just about every year, the newest series then goes at the front of the spiritual training that a person gets.

So at the present time, when people complete a discourse series, the next one they get is the latest first- or second-year series. They seem to never quite reach the point of receiving the discourses I wrote for those who are further along on the path.

That's why this person asked, "When do we get to see that other stuff you've written?" I'm curious too, actually.

"Accept what you have now," I answered. "The ECK writings, including our bible, *The Shariyat-Ki-Sugmad*, are very sacred teachings, as sacred as the holy scriptures of any of the religions of the world. But whatever outer writings you come across, you'll never find real truth in any of them, not even the ECK writings."

The Highest Truth

Some of you may wonder, *Why would he say something like that?* A Christian might think, *I can see why he'd say that about his bible, but our bible is different.*

No, it's not different. The highest truth is not written in any book, it's written in your heart. All the books in the world are useless unless they can help you open your heart.

Open your heart to what? To the love of God.

This is why we do the Spiritual Exercises of ECK. If you are into physical fitness, you run, walk, ride a bicycle, or find some kind of exercise that will make you more fit or keep you as fit as possible.

There are also exercises that we do to keep us fit spiritually.

The spiritual exercises open your heart to the Light and Sound of God, which is simply divine love, the love of God. When your heart opens to love, with it come wisdom and understanding.

Basically you find that none of these things can come from a book, no matter how holy.

Any kind of written matter suffers the indignity of translation, not just once but many times. The holy men of God may have spoken as they were moved by the Holy Ghost, but their words from long ago have gone through countless translations. With all the versions of the Christian Bible, it's pretty hard to figure out which words actually were spoken by those holy men.

Still, there are people even today who insist that their version of the Bible is literally true, and that the highest truth is written in that particular book.

Yet out of all the people who are studying the very same book, many have different ideas of the God that they are worshiping. It shows in the ways they treat each other. Some treat each other with respect, love, and grace, while others readily take advantage of their neighbor. So even if a book is very holy, what good is it if the person reading it is not very holy?

What can you do to become more spiritual? In ECK we do the Spiritual Exercises of ECK.

A very simple one is to sing the word *HU*.

Unexpected Rescue

A Catholic man in his early thirties wrote me a letter about his experience with the word *HU*.

He first heard about it from a friend, an ECKist, who had gone to one of the twelve-step programs with him. "Whenever you have a problem and you don't know what to do about it," the friend had said, "just sing HU silently to yourself." The ECKist explained that when you sing HU, you are opening your heart to the love and protection of God.

You also open yourself to wisdom, insight, compassion, and many of the other divine qualities that people look for.

The Catholic man had a hard time getting any sleep at night because of a recurring nightmare. It frightened him that he was a both an observer and a participant in whatever was going on in his inner worlds. He had no idea what was happening.

In this particular dream, he found himself in a barnyard facing a strange, snakelike creature with the head of a turkey.

The turkey's head was a deep, dark blue. It was one of those classic nightmarish things. He saw it as the personification of evil, or the devil. In ECK we call this negative force the Kal.

In each dream this creature came up to him to start a conversation. Somehow, the man knew that he had to tap the creature on the head with his fingers to keep it from hurting him. He didn't know how he knew, but he knew.

So every few minutes, no matter how frightened he was, he would reach out and go tap, tap, tap on the ghastly looking little head.

As both observer and participant while he was in this

7

inner world having a nightmare, he knew that his body was asleep in bed.

But he couldn't wake up.

Gratitude for HU

One night the Catholic man remembered the spiritual exercise his ECKist friend had told him about: When you're in trouble, sing HU.

So in the middle of his nightmare he began to sing HU.

All of a sudden the whole scene—the creature and the barnyard—just vanished in midair. He woke up abruptly, and though his heart was pounding, he realized he was no longer afraid.

Falling back to sleep, he found himself back in the barnyard, and there it was again; the snakelike creature with the head of a turkey. *What should I do now?* he wondered. Right away it came to him to simply chant HU, and once again the scene was gone.

He has been able to sleep much better since then.

In his letter, the Catholic man expressed his gratitude that this secret name of God, HU, was available to people of all religions.

This is why we made public the name HU. And this past year, many of you took the time to tell others about HU. They learned how to use the word, to sing it quietly or aloud in times of trouble.

The Catholic man wrote, "In the middle of my nightmares, I simply could not remember all the prayers that I had learned as a Christian, but I could remember HU." HU was simple, effective, and easy to remember. After he sang HU and the scene went away, he could then fall back on the Lord's Prayer and the exorcisms of his church to help him out.

Why Do People Have Nightmares?

In the ECK dream discourses which come with the first few years of membership in ECK, I explain many of the different aspects of dreams—what they are, where they come from, how to deal with them.

Often I get a letter from a parent who says, "My child doesn't get any sleep because of nightmares. What do I do?" You can take some comfort in the fact that the child will grow out of them, though it may take a couple of years.

Why do people have nightmares?

There are a lot of reasons, but the most essential one for children is that they are remembering incidents from one or more past lives. Usually it's from a past life that pertains directly to this one. They remember themselves as adults.

Children often talk to their parents about a past life. If the parent has no grounding in reincarnation or doesn't believe in it, the child is dismissed as having a wild imagination.

My parents dismissed me that way, saying, "Oh, he has such an imagination." Of course, I did, but that shouldn't invalidate my experience.

When your child has nightmares and you want to help, show him or her how to chant HU. It's a simple, effective way.

People who chant HU open themselves to the Light and Sound of God, which is divine love.

Straight Answers

An ECKist mentioned that a Christian friend back in her hometown asked her, "How can you be sure that the devil won't possess you when you look for this Light or listen for this Sound?" I tried to think of a graceful way to answer her, although in my writings I tend to be more direct, more confrontational.

When I see a false belief that people, especially members of ECK, have carried for years, I owe it to them—to you—to answer in a straightforward way. So I do.

If I told people who were not in ECK what I thought about certain aspects—rituals, practices, and beliefs—of other religions, some would be very upset with me. It is not my intention to upset anyone or to make them lose faith in their beliefs. Whatever your religion or belief, whether you are in ECK or not, it's what you need at the moment for this step in your journey home to God.

It is a valuable and important part of you because you are the sum of all your beliefs. This includes experiences from past lives.

We have a heritage much richer than a single lifetime, which explains why many children are born with a particular gift or knack for doing something. Some kids even come in knowing a certain language which their siblings do not. Parents who don't understand reincarnation simply say, "Oh, well, he or she didn't get it from us," and let it go at that. They have absolutely no idea where the child picked up that gift or talent.

Learning Spiritual Laws

Whenever I look at a child, I see a little adult. There is no reason to talk down to children when you realize that they actually are grownups who came back for another experience that they need on this leg of their spiritual journey.

Sometimes they come to learn the laws of power, other times to learn the laws of love.

A child of three, four, or five may have a very distinct personality, perhaps outgoing or adventurous. But when he reaches the age of eight to ten, he may suddenly turn shy and reserved. Looking back, you might notice that he doesn't seem like the same kid at all.

A very young child may still remember his past life, and often he'll talk about it.

A good question that a curious parent can ask a small child of two, three, or four is: What did you do when you were big? Don't be surprised if the child answers you in a very nonchalant way.

Once you leave a physical life, you then go to the next heaven, which we sometimes call the Astral Plane, to spend a little time or a lot of time. Or you may go to one of the other heavens, the second or third. St. Paul, as some of you know, spoke of the third heaven.

This is one of the places in the other worlds where you go to rest for a while and to learn some of the different facets of spiritual law, especially the Law of Love.

How Children Enter a New Life

After a period of time, you then come back here again, into a tiny baby form. And it's a prison. This perhaps is the hardest part of reincarnation. Just recently you were an adult in a functioning body. Now you try to move those little fingers and pick up things—you can't. You try to focus your eyes but the world is a blur. Sometimes it's a blur of black and white before it slowly becomes colors. Little by little the mind works to influence the brain in an effort to put it all together. It says, "Now sort out the light waves and try to make sense out of what you see."

Gradually forms begin to register. And pretty soon the infant begins to recognize Mommy and Daddy, knows

11

when the bottle's coming, and so on. A baby learns very quickly to put things into categories or files.

Placing something into a recognizable slot gets rid of fear and makes the world a more comfortable place.

An ECKist observed how her young child characterized things and put them into his own categories. At the age of ten months, he started to mimic certain sounds. Sometime after that, she noticed that every time they passed a body of water or a drinking fountain, he would say, "Mo."

One day she figured it out.

She had been teaching him to drink water from a glass. After each sip, she would say to him, "More." The child had taken the characteristics of this stuff in the glass and put it into the wrong file. He thought it was called "more." So anytime he saw water, he did his best to call it by name.

A child learns a little bit at a time. First it's the very basic things—how to identify the concrete objects in the world around him.

Eventually the child starts to learn how to do things, such as tying shoelaces. Nowadays, of course, you can get them with velcro straps, so they don't have to bother. When I was about four or five, I used to spend fifteen or twenty minutes trying to tie a shoelace. Finally I'd just give up, and my mother would do it. Now I just get shoes without laces.

How Do I Get God's Love?

Children then begin to learn the finer subtleties of getting along with other people. If they are fortunate enough to be surrounded by loving parents, they come to realize that as you get love, you naturally must give love.

12

Love is like water in that only so much can be poured into the glass. Before you can put more in, you have to let some out. If you don't keep giving out love, "mo" can't come in.

People often wonder, "How do I get God's love?" You get it by giving of yourself to others, in ways that you like to give.

Compassion for Others

We were caught up in mixed feelings at the ECKANKAR Spiritual Center this year. Being Minnesotans, naturally we wanted the Twins baseball team to get into the World Series—sort of.

But if they'd made it, there would have been no hotel rooms left over for the ECK seminar attendees.

So that led us to ponder the question: Does God really care whether the Twins win or lose? Last year we would have said yes. This year, no, because we needed the rooms for the ECK seminar.

Something else struck me as funny. A nineteen-year-old soldier down in Atlanta hung the Canadian flag with the maple leaf upside down. Though he didn't do it on purpose—he didn't know any better—I think our two countries were close to war.

North and South at war again, except it's way north and way south. My feeling was why not just let them work it out on the playing field. At least there would be some point to the World Series then. We could say, "This year we averted war with Canada—we lost in the World Series!"

People take affront so easily, sometimes gleaning the meanest meaning out of something the spiritual Masters may have put there for a reason.

They don't consider the possibility that an accident might be a blessing in disguise.

Of course, some of the Canadians in the audience are probably thinking, *Well, what if it had been your flag turned upside down? It means you're surrendering, doesn't it?* But with the Canadians preparing for a vote to decide whether or not to remain one nation, this incident might have served a purpose. For a few days the citizens had a reason to rally around the maple leaf. They may have realized that if they were willing to unite to stand behind their flag right side up, maybe their flag is pretty good after all.

In this Year of Graceful Living, have compassion for that soldier who turned the flag upside down. Long after we all forget about it, this little incident is going to trail him like a big load of bad karma, turning up in his military records wherever he goes for the rest of his life.

In some other lifetime, he'll probably come back as a Canadian, and if he gets the chance, may even hang the American flag upside down. Then with a little luck, everybody will play in the World Series and work that out peacefully.

The Funny Human Race

We're also in the middle of a big political campaign, which in some ways is better than the circus. I get a kick out of people who say, they are not going to vote unless they see somebody get 25 percent in the polls. These are the individual voters exercising their right to speak—but only if they can be part of a crowd.

We actually are a pretty funny family, we of the human race.

When we take ourselves too seriously or forget that

14

other people are Souls too—with the same rights that we expect for ourselves—this is when we get into family fights. One side or another raises their flag and goes off to war for their national honor.

When it's all over, those who are still alive have gotten a lot of experience. Then they all come back in another body to start the whole cycle over again.

In the 1860s America went through the Civil War. And some people haven't finished fighting that war yet. Though they keep coming back in other bodies, memories of the Civil War are still very strong in them. They still hate the blue or the grey. Often carrying strong feelings about the injustices done way back then, they'll fight at the drop of a hat. Then they all grow old, die, come back, and do it all again.

This is the kind of karma that is replayed over and over through reincarnation.

When these people come back and go through childhood again, it's no wonder some of them have nightmares— not only about the experiences they have suffered, but about the suffering they have caused others.

Spiritual School

All in all, Earth is still nothing more than a spiritual school. It was set up and designed by God so that each one of you, each Soul in this world, can learn more about becoming godlike and can become more like God.

This is the whole purpose of why you are here: to become more godlike.

Many people think they are here just to put in time until the trumpets blow on that last day. At that point, having lived a useless life here, they expect to be lifted up to some other world, apparently to live a useless life there.

15

No. The purpose of life is to become a Co-worker with God.

All the lives you have lived have been experiences designed for the polishing of Soul. Like it or not, as you sit here tonight, you are the best and highest spiritual being that you have ever been. If you take a look at yourself and don't like what you see, keep in mind that this is what you've made yourself. It's the sum of all your thoughts, feelings, and actions from before.

I mentioned to someone today that whenever people come to an ECK event, such as an introductory talk on the ECKANKAR teachings, understand that the reason they are there is because they are not completely satisfied with their own teaching. Otherwise they wouldn't be looking.

They may not be completely aware of how great their search is today. But Soul has heard and wants to go home to God.

It's just a matter of time—a week, a month, a year, fifty years, the next lifetime, whatever—it doesn't matter. If this is the lifetime in which the person finally says, "I have a sense that I've lived many times before, that I truly am the best that I've ever been, and I'm not real happy about it," then there may be something in the teachings of ECK for them.

Inner Teachings Come First

When people first run across ECKANKAR, or hear their first ECK talk, hear the word *HU*, they usually are already familiar with it. Why?

Because people who come to the outer teachings have often been getting the inner teachings for years, even in previous lifetimes. In this lifetime they may struggle, they may fight the ECK, but eventually Soul will return.

Soul is the true being that you are. You are Soul.

When Soul hears with the spiritual ears and sees with the spiritual eyes, It will return. For It knows that this is the place where It can find the love of God and the purest stream, like the living water.

Graceful Living

Two weeks before a seminar, the ECK, the Holy Spirit, sometimes makes known certain things It wants me to bring out in my talks. Then I wonder how to bring up a subject like that, to make it useful to others.

As the time draws closer to the first talk on Friday night, I can hardly wait; I want to find out what's going on too!

Enjoy yourself at the spiritual new year's party tonight, because Soul is a happy being.

When you are with others, realize that they too are Lights of God who are also trying to find their way home to a better, happier, more graceful life.

ECK Worldwide Seminar, Minneapolis, Minnesota,
Friday, October 23, 1992

When your goal is spiritual freedom, you will find your-self moving into those areas where you can best express yourself, whether you are a man, a woman, black, white, yellow, red, Christian, ECKist, Hindu, whatever.

2

Female ECK Masters, Equality, and Past-Life Therapy

One question that comes up occasionally is, Why do the ECK teachings speak more about male ECK Masters than female?

At least 50 percent of you are probably thinking, *Yeah, good question!*

The ECK Masters who are in charge of the Temples of Golden Wisdom here on the physical plane, as well as on the other planes, have served terms in the past as the Mahanta, the Living ECK Master. One of the tenets of ECK is that whoever will become the Mahanta, the Living ECK Master reincarnates into this life in the male form.

Having a Choice

People under the hand of karma often don't have a choice in whether they come back as male or female. But as you go farther on the spiritual path, you have a say in what body form you will take when you come into the next life.

Sometimes people come here to work with a certain aspect of the ECK.

One aspect of ECK is power, the other is love. And they

are not necessarily separate. A person might gravitate more toward one than the other because that is the polishing that this particular Soul will benefit from most in this particular lifetime.

Why are there more pictures of male ECK Masters available? Because all the Mahantas, the Living ECK Masters in history were male. This is SUGMAD's plan.

SUGMAD's Plan

Why did SUGMAD set up this kind of plan for the polishing or purifying of Soul? It's not for me to say; that's just the way it is.

You have to understand, the Mahanta, the Living ECK Master reincarnates in a male form to undergo the tests of Mastership. At any given time there are numerous people who come into the male form to do this.

They have earned the right, and they have made the choice. It's not just one or the other, it's both: earned the right and made the choice.

Some males who have not earned the right but have named themselves as candidates for mastership are just working under illusion. It's a fantasy in their own mind when they say, "I'm the next Mahanta, the Living ECK Master." To do this is not part of the spiritual order or the SUGMAD's will.

It's something they made up themselves because it strokes the feathers of ego.

Literally hundreds and thousands of other Souls have come here, either in male or female form, and become ECK Masters after having passed the tests. Occasionally I will mention a person in the ECK writings, either male or female, who has reached the heights of Mastership. I don't do it often, if only to keep things simple.

20

Split Attention

As a student of history, I think it can get confusing to have too many high spiritual beings running around in a religious teaching.

The saints adopted by the early Catholic church were takeoffs of the ancient Greek and Roman gods and goddesses. Pretty soon the people were looking to this or that saint, the saint of travel or whatever, for everything. The Christian church became so splintered that you couldn't really be sure if the central figure was the savior, Jesus, Mary, Saint This, or Saint That.

The people took on so many different saints, whom they looked upon as gods, that they split within themselves the focus of spiritual striving.

This split attention sent them in too many different directions to ever get anywhere.

Religions and Their Gods

At one time the ancient Greeks had Zeus, Athena, and a number of other gods. The Romans later shuffled things around and renamed some of the gods—Jupiter, Apollo, and so on—blurring the edges of the Greek gods. There is such a large army of gods in religious history that it's sometimes hard to keep them straight.

The Roman Empire began to expand its borders until it extended as far as England. Groups of people within every local area had started out with their main deities—gods of harvest, fertility, or weather. They were all similar, but each region had different names for them. But as the Roman pagan religion spread from one locale to another, something interesting happened. The people who lived under the safety of the Roman umbrella and traveled from one part of the empire to another encountered so many different gods that they began to lose track.

Christianity came to the scene just about the time the Roman Empire was expanding.

One of the reasons its doctrine of monotheism spread so fast was because it simplified things. It combined the whole slew of gods and goddesses into the teaching of one God.

At that point, when a traveler brought the message "There is but one God," the people were relieved. They no longer had to risk getting the gods of the southwest part of the empire mixed up with those of the northeast. None of that occurred anymore.

Now they only had to keep track of the Christian saints.

Real Masters

In ECK we have the ECK Masters. Many of you who are doing the spiritual exercises do meet them on the inner planes on occasion. Therefore, you can say, "Yes, I do know about Rebazar Tarzs" or "I do know about Fubbi Quantz. They are real." There are also cases where people met these Masters before they even came into ECK.

Only after they got into ECK did they realize that the person who came to them on the inner planes was Rebazar Tarzs, Fubbi Quantz, Peddar Zaskq, or one of the other ECK Masters.

Today we are setting the example for how the teachings of ECK will be taught in the future, how our children will teach their children. It is now that we have to say, "For those of you who can find the ECK Masters on the inner planes, fine. After all, that's what the secret teachings are about. But for those who can't, the teachings remain secret."

This is why I encourage all ECKists to do the spiritual

exercises. The outer teachings, where these exercises are given in great abundance, are only to help you get to the inner planes.

This is where you can find the real teachings of ECK; this is where you can meet the ECK Masters, male and female.

It is with the intent to keep things simple that most of the focus in ECK is on the Mahanta, the Living ECK Master. The ECK Masters who are in the foreground, such as Rebazar Tarzs, have a specific mission to fulfill. And that is to help the Mahanta, the Living ECK Master of the times.

To Give Is to Live

These other ECK Masters, the males that we talk about in the ECK teachings, have already served their term sometime in the past as the Mahanta, the Living ECK Master. They know what the duties of this position entail. There is no envy, no striving to be the big cheese.

Those who have reached Mastership simply want to serve the SUGMAD; that's all they care about.

There is nothing in it for them—except life.

To give is to live, and this is why I talk about service. If you want to live more spiritually, then you must give more and more in the way of service to all life.

Look for Spiritual Freedom

Today we have the equality issue. Races, sexes, and religions are striving for equality. I'm not saying it's unnecessary, but it's a fad. In the long range of history, it won't matter.

My point is this: Don't waste your time striving to be equal.

Do you really want to be equal with the rest of the human race who are in bondage to karma? Do you want to be equal to that? Is that your goal?

I would rather look for spiritual freedom. It's a whole different thing.

Don't look for equality, look for spiritual freedom. When your goal or aim in life is spiritual freedom, you will find yourself moving into those areas where you can best express yourself, whether you are a man, a woman, black, white, yellow, red, Christian, ECKist, Hindu, whatever.

You cannot find the full expression for your life by setting your sights on equality.

Equality

Again, you don't want to be equal with the human race and its load of karma. If you do, this path is not for you. Set your sights on spiritual freedom. Leave equality for others.

I'm not saying that you shouldn't fight for equality or participate in the efforts. This is what you can do outwardly. If you have strong feelings about how many male representatives you have in government, and you want more women, well, then, vote. Or join committees where you can help to get more women elected to office.

These things don't just happen.

There is an imbalance in the governments of the world today—so many men, so few women. But in the countries that allow the citizens to vote, as in the United States, at least 50 percent of the voters are women. Don't sit around and rail at the men for being in charge. You've got the vote; do something about it. Why not elect more women to public office?

This is what you can do out here.

But as I mentioned before, this whole thing is a fad, and as such, it's shortsighted and short-lived. Keep your vision on spiritual freedom, not on equality.

Because if you set your sights on equality, you're aiming too low.

You may or may not agree, but do you see my point?

Past-Life Therapy

Someone asked me by letter, "Can an ECKist become a doctor who does regressive therapy?"

I have no problem with it. A healing profession is a field of service, and anyone who enters it wants to do some good. Something that often goes with regressive therapy is hypnosis. As for my position on hypnotism, when it's used as a medical tool, I have no problem with that either.

Problems arise when people play with it to control others for their own purposes.

There are many different ways to use hypnotism, including mass hypnosis and other forms which I am against. On the other hand, when it is used ethically by someone in the medical profession to help heal people, to help them come to an understanding about themselves, I have no problem with it.

However, an ECKist who wants to become a doctor and practice regressive hypnosis should not promote it as a part of the teachings of ECK. If they want to draw on other ECKists for their business, I would discourage it. Again, we're aiming too low.

Regressive therapy involves hypnotizing someone to

help them see past lives or remember events from their childhood. It's OK for people who are in a crisis. By all means, go to a psychotherapist if that's who you feel can give you the help you need. Psychotherapy is another way that the ECK has provided for healing.

A Fuller Understanding of Past Lives

For an ECKist who is well balanced, I would suggest doing the Spiritual Exercises of ECK.

Undertake the self-discipline to learn how to go into the other worlds with the Mahanta and, with his guidance, see your past lives. This will give you a fuller understanding of the experience than hypnotherapy.

Regressive therapy works like this: A person has a problem with alcohol or perhaps some phobia such as fear of heights, fear of going outside, fear of men, of women, this sort of thing. So he goes to a psychotherapist who uses hypnotism to take him back to a past life. The images then bring about some realization — "Ah! The reason I hate Uncle Jim or Aunt Helen now is because they abused me in a past life."

In many cases, then, the patient of the psychotherapist has gotten a degree of healing. He can say, "Oh, I feel much better now that I know why I can't stand Uncle Jim or Aunt Helen."

What the patient may not realize is that when the psychotherapist hypnotizes him, neither he nor the hypnotist has control over which past lives come forward on the screen of the mind.

The censor is in charge.

The censor is the part of the subconscious mind that has taken it upon itself to decide what's good for you and what's not. It is also the dream censor.

If anything in your past lives would show you how to break away from the bonds of Kal, the negative power, the censor won't let you see it. The censor has a stake in this: being a part of the lower mind, its job is to keep Soul trapped in the lower worlds.

The dream censor is not going to tell you what you need to know to advance spiritually.

In some cases, the psychotherapist may also have a bias. He has a mortgage, a car payment, and a desire to live the good life. So even if he suspects the cause of your problem, he may not want to tell you any more than the censor does. He may not want to say, "You abused people before, and that's why you're abused now."

If he were to lay it on the line, the patient might not come back. How does the therapist make the mortgage and the car payments then?

What I'm getting at is that sometimes it's not a level playing field when a past life opens up under hypnosis by a psychotherapist.

At best, you get just enough to keep you in the control of the Kal.

There may be exceptions, of course, but in the case histories I've read, where someone glimpses a past life and sees incidents in which they were the victim of abuse, the person comes out of it feeling very self-righteous. Very, very seldom does psychotherapy reveal a past-life experience that makes a patient say, "The reason I was an abused child in this lifetime is because I caused it first."

I'm not saying this makes it right. When people abuse children, there is a law to pay, and this is as it should be. These laws keep the social balance here on earth, which is also part of the spiritual structure.

The social framework is part of the polishing of

Soul. You cannot take advantage of others in the spiritual worlds.

Victim Consciousness

Just because you go to a psychotherapist and experience seeing a past life, you don't necessarily have the full answer. It's doubtful that you would see all the lifetimes in which you abused others. Because you couldn't handle it.

People who adopt the attitude "I'm a victim, I'm abused" might as well be running around in a dark room with their eyes shut.

They're so self-righteous, so right; the only reason their life is bad is because of somebody else.

Self-Responsibility

The bottom line is, they refuse to take responsibility for themselves.

I find fault with any healing method that says, "We have healed you," yet does not explain at the same time that you are responsible for your life, not someone else. The abuse you endured is the result of the time that you once abused this person.

Again, this does not justify their actions under the social laws. Abusers pay. But spiritual law decrees that you can only get out of life what you have put into it.

A Clearer Focus

I hope I got some points across about why there are mostly male ECK Masters in our teachings. To keep things simple and because these ECK Masters served past terms as the Mahanta, the Living ECK Master. The

SUGMAD chooses the male form because of the positive atoms.

This is not to say that the female form is made up purely of negative atoms, but those are the preponderance of atoms in the female form. You chose this before you came into this life.

Or you may have been given a certain form to enter because that body—male or female, or a certain color or religion—could provide exactly the opportunity you need for the greatest spiritual unfoldment in this lifetime.

As for abuse and past-life therapy, how far does an abused person go before taking responsibility for himself or herself?

These are questions I wanted to bring a little more into focus for you. I wanted to touch on these subjects to bring out one main point: Self-responsibility is the key to spiritual freedom.

Initiates' Meeting, ECK Worldwide Seminar, Minneapolis, Minnesota, Saturday, October 24, 1992

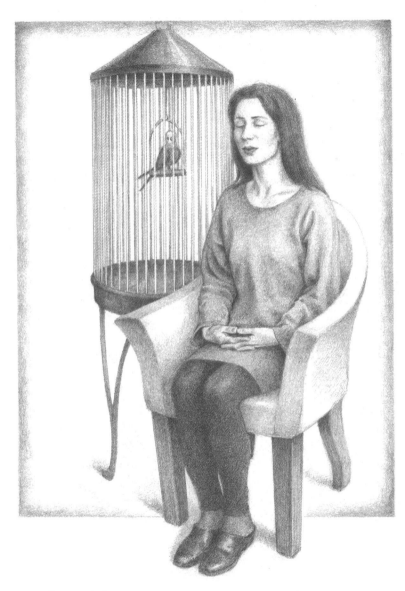

The quickest way to put your state of consciousness in the heart of God is to sing HU. Just sing HU-U-U-U to yourself a few times. You'll notice that something changes.

3

About Dreams and Things

Two weeks ago I had lunch with a few of the ECK initiates who work at the Temple of ECK. They brought me a very special gift.

They had gone to the woods on the Temple grounds, and underneath a red oak tree they found some fallen acorns. After gathering up a bunch of them, they very carefully washed them off—can you believe it?—then placed them in a nice little basket and handed it to me over lunch.

"That's very kind of you," I said. "I think I'll have one."

"We brought them for your squirrels," they said. "I don't think you want to eat them," one of the ECKists added. When somebody tells you that, of course, you have to do it anyway.

I went home and tried to remember how we used to open hickory nuts when I was a kid. We would store them in a milk can in the garage loft for half the winter. Once the nuts were dried out, my brothers and I would climb up the ladder and fill our pockets. Then we'd take them to the barn, lay them out on the floor, and crush them with our heels.

I did the same with one of the acorns, then put some

31

of the fruit in my mouth. It was the bitterest thing I'd ever tasted. The ECKist who warned me against eating them knew what she was talking about—she had probably tried some herself.

Feeding the Squirrels

When it was time to feed the squirrels, I took the birdseed outside and poured it into their two dishes, then put a little bit extra on the patio for the birds. Curious to see how our squirrels would deal with the acorns, I dropped a handful into each of their dishes.

These were city squirrels raised on birdseed. As far as I knew, they wouldn't even recognize an acorn.

I went in the house and stood by the window to watch. The first squirrel approached the dish, cautiously picked up an acorn, and went absolutely crazy. He jumped up and down, ran around in a circle, then tore off across the lawn.

Up in the trees the other squirrels, noticing all the excitement down there, had to see what was going on. They ran down and found the acorns, then promptly went crazy too.

They each took an acorn and scurried across the lawn in a different direction.

I had always heard that squirrels were very industrious, burying the acorns so that they would have food in the winter. Let me tell you, our squirrels will never find their acorns again. They have no idea where they put the things.

They ran back to the dishes several times for more acorns, which they carried around for a while before dropping them in the grass. They didn't even dig holes. When they'd emptied the dishes, they ran back out on the lawn and tried to find them.

In the twenty minutes I watched, only one squirrel found one acorn, probably because he stubbed his toe on it.

Eventually they went through the whole basket of acorns. I put some out every day, fewer and fewer as we got near the bottom of the supply. That was how I broke the news to them that, hey, the acorns runneth low.

Contemplation Is Appreciation

While you are here for the seminar, or at any time in the future, I would like to invite you to walk the contemplation trails on the grounds of the Temple of ECK. It's like taking a nice long walk in the country.

Another word for contemplation is *appreciation.* As you walk the trails in contemplation, think about all the reasons you have to be grateful.

Think about the gifts in your life that have come from God, from the Holy Spirit, that make this life worth living. Think about the adventures that are coming, and be grateful for the strength to meet tomorrow.

Walk the trails and enjoy the scenery. There are fourteen contemplation points along the way, each with a sign offering a passage from the ECK writings. Read the passage, and think about it.

Then walk on and appreciate the gift of life.

True contemplation is reflecting on the blessings of God in your life. It's not complex, there are many ways to do it, and it certainly will enrich you.

Bank Robbery

An initiate was reading one of the ECK books, *Unlocking the Puzzle Box,* Mahanta Transcripts, Book 6, and feeling grateful for the blessings that had come into her

33

life. She got so caught up in the book that she was a little bit late leaving for an errand to the bank. Finally she put the ECK book aside and got in her car.

The bank was just down the street and around the corner. Parking her car, she tried to enter the building but found that the doors were locked.

Through the window she saw a cluster of policemen mingling with the clerks and customers. Someone told her the bank had been robbed.

It occurred to her that if she had left home on her original schedule, she would have ended up right in the middle of a bank robbery — an experience she didn't really need. She managed to miss the event because something in the ECK book had caught her attention and caused her to read a little bit longer than she had planned.

Totally Absorbed

It's always flattering to hear from someone who has had a real insight because of something I said. This makes a speaker feel good.

This morning I spoke to the initiates in a private meeting, explaining why in ECKANKAR we talk mostly about the male ECK Masters and not too often about the female ECK Masters. I went into this at great length, wondering if anyone really understood the message.

Later I learned that one of the ECKists, leaving the auditorium after the talk, was lost deeply in thought as she walked over to the ladies' room.

At least, that's where she planned to go. Instead, she looked up to find herself in the men's room — among some very surprised men.

Like I said, it's always flattering to hear that someone became so absorbed in my talk.

Learning Grace

Another ECK initiate, a schoolteacher, told me about an experience she'd had ten years ago. Before she left for work one morning, she went into contemplation to ask a question of the Inner Master.

The Inner Master is one of the fundamentals in ECK. This is the inner side of the present spiritual leader of ECKANKAR.

The ECK books are simply to show people how to go inside themselves, into the pureness of their heart, where they can get answers directly from the Inner Master about things of a spiritual nature, insights to help them in their life.

Her question was, "What quality will help me grow the most spiritually?"

She thought the answer probably would be love, or perhaps getting more joy out of life—she wasn't really sure.

In contemplation the answer came through, very softly and gently: "Grace."

Soon it was time to leave for work. Though she didn't have enough time to look in the dictionary for the full definition of grace, she decided it must mean an attitude of thankfulness. *Living with gratitude for the blessings of God,* she thought. *That must be grace.*

Still thinking this over, she got in her car and headed for the school where she taught.

As soon as she pulled onto the highway, a huge truck unexpectedly cut her off and almost drove her off the road. It took her a minute to get over the shock, but as she started to calm down, she became very angry at the truck driver.

Suddenly she realized that she was allowing her anger to take over.

"Now wait a minute," she said. "I just got the answer in contemplation that the quality that would help me the most in my spiritual unfoldment is grace." Letting go of her anger, she was able to consider the possibility that the driver never even saw her. She gave thanks for the fact that she hadn't been injured or killed in what could have been a very serious accident.

A little farther down the highway she caught up to the truck. It was moving very slowly up a hill. As she pulled around it, something made her glance over.

There on the side of the truck, in great big letters, was the word *GRACE*.

This is an example of the waking dreams that we talk about in ECKANKAR. Sometimes the Holy Spirit will arrange for an outer confirmation of what was revealed in your inner worlds, in your heart. This connection between the inner and outer is what we call the waking dream.

In this case, the woman got the message from the Inner Master that the most important quality she could develop was grace.

Out on the highway, instead of giving in to anger, she gave thanks. Her gratitude gave her the awareness to look over at the truck. And the word she saw confirmed the answer she had gotten in contemplation just a little while before.

The ECK, or Holy Spirit, uses any number of ways to bring you answers or insights about the right thing to do.

It brings confirmation into your life in times of doubt.

Copper Coins

An ECKist had to make a decision about her future. In less than a year, she would have accumulated enough time to leave the company she worked for. On the other hand, she wondered if it would be wiser to work a few more years and put aside a little extra money.

She really didn't know what to do.

One evening she had a conversation with the ECK, the Holy Spirit. "Got a little test for you," she said. "Three weeks before I'm to retire, show me a little copper coin that has a hole near the edge." She had selected an item that was not too common, yet something that you possibly could expect to see.

Then she put it out of her mind, not expecting to see this sign from the ECK for at least another eleven months.

A week later she received a gift catalog in the mail. Flipping through it, she spotted a pair of copper-coin earrings. Each of the coins had a hole punched near the edge.

"No fair," she said. "It doesn't count if it's in a catalog."

Three weeks after that, her employer offered certain employees early retirement, complete with a cash bonus so that they could afford to do it. Though it came eleven months earlier than she'd expected, she realized that the Holy Spirit had given her an insight into the best course to take, in a way that she could understand.

These are the little things that happen constantly, not only in the life of an ECKist. But I think they come more often in the life of an ECKist. You are looking for these insights because you realize that this is how the Holy Spirit works in everyday life. You know that the kind of miracles reported in biblical times still happen today, all the time.

All you need to do to recognize and benefit from these gifts of the Holy Spirit is to open your consciousness.

In ECK, of course, we open the consciousness through the Spiritual Exercises of ECK, such as singing HU.

Guillotine Dream

A gentleman from Canada had an experience that involves the dream state more than waking dreams.

Some years ago, just as he was coming into ECK, he lay down on the couch after a hard day's work to watch TV. Soon he fell asleep.

He woke up to find an old black-and-white movie about the French Revolution just coming to an end.

Still groggy from sleep, he watched the final scene: A group of nobles were being led to the guillotine. Some lived up to their nobility, not even blinking an eye, while others screamed, kicked, and cursed their way right to the end.

Mentally he began to play with the idea of himself in that role. If he had lived during the French Revolution, how would he have dealt with being dragged to the guillotine? It was just an idle thought.

That night in the dream state, the Dream Master, who is also the Inner Master, began showing him the same black-and-white film he had seen while he was awake.

"In a second you're going to be in that movie," the Master said.

"But I don't want to be in the French Revolution," the man protested.

"You have to go there," the Master said. "But you will understand later."

Suddenly the dreamer found himself a participant in the movie, a condemned noble being dragged to the guillotine by two revolutionaries. A part of him felt ashamed at the realization that he was kicking and cursing every step of the way. They forced him up the steps to the platform where he was to be beheaded and locked him in place. The blade made a whistling sound on its way down.

Just before the blade struck his neck, he found himself out of the body, standing next to the Dream Master.

"Whenever you have a thought," the Master said, "it has life."

Thoughts Have Life

People generally don't realize that without the protection of divine love, even the most idle thought creates a karmic situation that needs to be resolved sometime later.

In ECK we learn to protect ourself by singing HU.

If you have one of these thoughts and you're aware of it, just say, "Whoops, I really don't need that experience," and sing HU.

People constantly pick up these little bits of karma that have to be worked out at some point in their daily life, either in this lifetime or in another. One of the advantages of being in ECK is that you can work out much of the karma in the dream state. Then you don't have to go through the wear and tear out here in the physical body.

Yes, there are lessons out here; life doesn't necessarily become easier for someone who is in ECK.

But the lessons that come outwardly will be absolutely necessary for you, only those you cannot get in any other way.

First Connection

A woman from Australia, whose first connection with ECK was through the dream state, recently wrote to request information about the ECK teachings. In her letter she explained how her introduction to the teachings came about.

She had shared a large home with her fiancé for four years, and when the relationship broke up, she moved to a dingy little apartment. Emotionally, it was a very difficult period for her.

"Can I do something to brighten up the place?" she asked her new landlord.

"Sure, go ahead," he said. She then proceeded to clean and paint until she had turned the apartment into a warm haven from the stress of the working world.

Several months later, many of the belongings that she had brought with her from the big house were still in boxes. Now that the apartment was fixed up, she decided to begin the tedious task of unpacking.

In a box of books she came across *The Flute of God* by Paul Twitchell.

That's strange, she thought. She hadn't bought it, didn't remember ever seeing it before, and had never heard of ECKANKAR.

It was an earlier printing of *The Flute of God.* The cover was a pretty, pale yellow, the same color she had just painted her apartment. Turning the book over, she saw on the back cover a picture of the ECK Master Paul Twitchell.

The woman immediately recognized him. He was the man who had come to her in her dreams for the past nine months.

Just Accept the Love

The first night it happened, she was asleep when suddenly she got the feeling that someone else was in the room. Opening her eyes, she saw a light that grew brighter and brighter until it filled the entire room. In the center of this light stood a being, the man she later learned was Paul Twitchell.

He came to the side of the bed and, without touching her, held his hands above her. The power of the love of God she felt in him took away all her fear.

"Who are you?" she asked. "What are you doing here?"

"Be quiet," he answered. "Just accept the love." And then he was gone.

He came back several more times during those months she was going through that rough emotional time in her life. When she came across the book and saw his face on the cover, she was struck by the fact that the book said he had died in 1971. Yet she knew he was alive; he had come and talked with her.

That's when she decided to write me to learn more about ECKANKAR.

Her letter had one date at the top. Ten days later she had added a note at the bottom: "You'll notice that I didn't mail this letter after I finished writing the first part."

She explained that a few days after she wrote the letter to me, Paul Twitchell came to her again, surrounded by light.

He said, "You now have the Light and Sound of God," and he left. After meeting Paul and experiencing the Light of God, she knew that the power of love had more meaning in her life than she had ever realized.

She knew she had to send her letter to ECKANKAR and find out what this was all about.

An Individual Path

Another person commented to me, "There must be as many different ways to come to ECKANKAR as there are individuals in ECK."

This is true: ECK is an individual path made just for you.

Although the outer teachings cannot tailor the spiritual clothing closely enough to fit each person individually, they do provide a gateway, a stepping-stone into the other worlds. This puts you in more direct contact with the source of love, where each of you can get the insights and wisdom you need at that particular moment in your life.

The true ECK teachings fit each individual, because the help you find on the spiritual planes is infinite. The Holy Spirit can work with you, as a spark of God, in exactly the way that's right for you.

Dreams, which are an important part of the ECK teachings, work in a number of ways. The ECK-Vidya is an aspect of the teachings that helps you know the future. This is not to say that being in ECKANKAR means you'll have a dream every night that tells you exactly what tomorrow's going to bring.

It would be a very dull life, let me assure you.

The ECK-Vidya is for special occasions, when you are at a certain important crossroads in life where you need extra help or extra love or support. This is when your dreams may bring a message that gives you comfort, strength, insight, patience, compassion, or whatever you need.

Temple Technique

One of the Temples of Golden Wisdom here on the physical plane is the Temple of ECK in Chanhassen, Minnesota. Any of you who visit will find that it has a special character, a presence of its own. That presence is the love of God.

Go there with an open mind, without any ideas or notions about what this presence should be. Look around, listen to the tour guide, and just be there.

Later, if you are ever in need of spiritual help, imagine yourself back at the Temple.

Do this at some quiet time—in your private moments of contemplation or at bedtime. Ask the question that is on your mind, that you need help with, and then just go to sleep. Often you'll wake up in the morning with an entirely different view of the situation.

The Temple is here for a spiritual purpose, and it's not just for ECKists. It's for people of all religions. You don't have to leave your religion and become a member of ECK to enjoy the benefits of the ECK Temple; just come.

No one there will be pushy; it's not our way. The missionary effort in ECK is unlike that of most religious groups in that we don't feel the need to push the blessings of God, as we imagine them to be, upon other people. To do that is to take on the burdens of these Souls, and the burdens are especially heavy when you push somebody who is not ready into your religion. You become responsible for that person.

An ECKist with any degree of awareness at all will not push others to come to ECK.

If they come before they're ready, you'll have to help carry them along. And believe me, no matter how strong you think you are, you are not strong enough for that.

Operating Room

A doctor in Nigeria who does the spiritual exercises regularly often meets with the Dream Master. One night in a dream he found himself in an operating room,

43

about to perform surgery on a patient. In vivid detail he saw his scalpels and other surgical instruments laid out in front of him.

As he began to work on the patient, he found a hernia.

He thought the problem was solved until suddenly an inner voice told him, "Look a little further."

Exploring a little further, he found that besides the hernia there was an obstruction off to the side. Step-by-step, in great detail and in full awareness, he went through the entire operation. As soon as it was completed, he awoke and sat straight up in bed.

What was that all about? he wondered.

The next morning the ECKist got a call from his brother—also a doctor—who needed some advice on a patient.

"I don't quite know what to make of his symptoms," he told the ECKist. He proceeded to describe a condition exactly like that of the patient in the ECKist's dream the night before.

Without wasting a minute, the ECKist said, "Take the patient straight to the hospital and set up the operating room."

He left home immediately to meet his brother there.

At the hospital he began to perform the operation exactly as he had in his dream, right to the smallest detail.

Because the Inner Master had tipped him off the night before, he knew just where to look to find the obstruction that had caused the problem. He was able to remove it.

If he hadn't found and removed the obstruction, it would have led to severe complications, perhaps even the death of the patient.

How to Be an Open Vehicle

When the Inner Master, the Mahanta, works with an ECKist, down the road there may be benefits for someone who has never heard of ECKANKAR—like the patient in this case.

You never know when the Holy Spirit may tap you on the shoulder and ask you to be a channel for It. These experiences come often to the person who does the spiritual exercises and keeps his or her heart open.

There are others who don't bother with the spiritual exercises because they don't have the personal discipline. These are often the same people who complain that ECK doesn't work for them. Their complaints tell me that they are not putting their heart into their search for God; they're not willing to do the disciplines.

Help in Critical Times

This morning I mentioned some of the merits of psychotherapy. If you feel you need to go to a psychiatrist or some other medical professional to help you through a critical time in your emotional life, by all means, go to that person.

The Holy Spirit has allowed for many different areas of healing. Take what's available. When your health is in a critical state, seek out the person best able to help you deal with it, whether it's a psychotherapist or a dentist.

Someone suffering with a toothache two hundred years ago had no choice but to live with it. When the pain became unbearable, the dentist didn't fill the tooth, he pulled it. His tools included a pair of pliers, a good grip, and alcohol to help you get through it. That was

45

state-of-the-art dentistry in those days. Most of us now live in better times as far as treatment of the physical body is concerned.

The same applies to treatment of the emotional body; there are doctors who can help now. But in a way, psychotherapy today is at the stage of dentistry two hundred years ago.

The psychotherapist who uses hypnosis to show a patient past lives has no idea which one will come up on the screen.

Dream Censor

There is an element in dreams we call the censor, which is part of the unconscious mind. It will not allow anything to come to the awareness of the average human being that will destroy his self-image, even if it's for his own good.

This is especially true of a very vain person. The censor will not allow information to come through that tells the peacock he's actually a crow.

This is why the help available professionally is not the fullest help that one might expect, although it may be a lot better than anything else you could do right now.

But if you are not in a crisis emotionally, I would prefer that you take the time and trouble to do the Spiritual Exercises of ECK.

The dream censor will not show you the inner experience or the past life that might help you most spiritually. It will show you only enough to get you by, to make you feel a little bit better. It will give you a bit of an understanding that might help you overcome gluttony or lose some of your fears about people, heights, and so on.

The censor will show you a time when you were the

victim of abuse. It will not tell you about the times you were the abuser who started the ball rolling in some past life.

But the Mahanta, the Dream Master, will.

The Mahanta will bring to your attention those past lives that will be for your good spiritually. And when you receive a spiritual healing, this will also take care of the emotional and mental part. Very often there also will be an improvement in your physical circumstances.

A psychotherapist, at best, can only heal on an emotional level, not on a spiritual level. He is not a spiritual healer. But he's a lot better than nothing.

All Healing Is from God

I want to encourage you to recognize the many different ways the Holy Spirit, or the ECK, has provided to make your life better.

Whatever healing profession you need, go there. Some of the religions today still say, "We will only get our healing naturally." So their loved ones die, simply because they will not seek out the available treatment.

Where do these people think the doctors and scientists got the information to bring about healing? It all comes from God, from the Holy Spirit.

In this sense, all healing is from God.

Don't be so vain as to think that, in your great human wisdom, you know it is best to select this method of healing but not that one.

Thoughts are things. As surely as you have an opinion, especially about something you say you will have nothing to do with, you've set up the situation that will send you to exactly that kind of doctor. I can almost guarantee it.

Still, in ECK you don't have to live in fear that every time you leave home, you'll step on an ant and have that to worry about.

Just surround yourself with God's love.

The quickest way to put your state of consciousness in the heart of God is to sing HU. Just sing HU-U-U-U to yourself a few times. You'll notice that something changes.

Good Friends

A woman told me of an experience she'd had before she found ECKANKAR. She and her mother were very good friends, which is not always the case between parent and child. It's very heartening when two people have a close, warm relationship where the love and respect comes through.

One day the woman stopped in to visit her mother but caught her at a bad time.

"I'm in a real hurry," the mother said. "I have an appointment with the eye doctor." They only had a few minutes to chat.

The mother had always been afraid of death, wondering how it would come about. But on that particular day she said to her daughter, "You know, I've learned something over the years. Sometimes it's better not to know what's coming, because then you don't worry about it."

Two hours later she was killed in a car accident on her way home from the eye doctor.

As the daughter struggled to understand why this had happened, a message kept coming gently into her mind: *Your mother will teach you more through her death than she did throughout her life.* The daughter didn't quite know what this meant.

Over the next two years she searched for answers. During that time she met with her mother in the dream state a number of times.

The experiences were so real that she knew she was there and her mother was alive, well, and happy. Every time they met, the daughter brought back a feeling of love and joy.

Still she kept wondering, *What is all this about? What is the meaning of life? Where is my mother? Why am I so happy when I see her, even though I don't understand what's going on?*

The woman enrolled in some courses on religion. One day in class the teacher announced, "We have a guest speaker today who is going to talk to us about ECKANKAR."

During the talk she began to get certain insights into what was happening in the dream state and how she was able to have actual meetings with her mother.

She began to understand that Soul lives forever.

Soul Lives Forever

Soul takes on a different body in each life, drops it when the time is over, then takes on still another body. This goes on until the time when Soul becomes purified enough to serve as a Co-worker with God, at which point that Soul no longer has to return to earth unless the individual chooses to do so.

Why would anyone choose to come back to earth?

Why would we choose to be born in a helpless little baby's body, to once again have to work through all the misconceptions of the religion of the family we are born in until, in young adulthood or so, we come to an awareness of ourself as Soul? Why go through it again?

To help other people find God. To help other people find the way to the Holy Spirit.

Many of you have done the same thing. You came quite far spiritually in the past, and in this lifetime you are going for the final polishing. As you do, you realize that you must serve God with love.

How We Serve God

This doesn't mean you have to serve in a dull, dreary way by doing things you don't want to do. You use your talents to do what you love doing.

One of our members from Singapore, for example, is a very skilled illustrator who worked for four years to convert our holy book, *The Shariyat-Ki-Sugmad,* the Way of the Eternal, into comic-book format.

When he offered to do this, I wondered how he was going to take those words and make them into images. But he did a nice job. He was able to get to the heart of *The Shariyat.* And after he finished, he was offered a job at Disney Studios, which he accepted.

You serve God by being open to the Holy Spirit and going about your life. And if someone needs help, you help where you can.

Then, when people later find ECK, in some way you may have played a small part.

No two people have the same consciousness, no matter how close they may be. Everyone in this room tonight has come to ECK by a unique route, because each of you is unique, one of a kind; God made you, then threw away the mold. But the form keeps changing and always will as Soul expands in awareness.

The person you are now is entirely different from the child you were years ago. You're not the same person anymore, because you have a different consciousness today.

May the blessings be.

ECK Worldwide Seminar, Minneapolis, Minnesota, Saturday, October 24, 1992

If there is something you need to know, you have to be of a mind to ask. Then you need to learn how to listen and how to see.

4

One Step Away (A Focus on God)

A staff member at the Temple of ECK has a cat she calls Calamity Jane who usually comes home around 10:30 each night. Recently the cat stayed out all night.

When the ECKist heard a noise outside at 5:00 the next morning, she opened the door to find two dead mice lying on the doorstep—a gift from Calamity Jane. The ECKist felt a little sad seeing them there; she would just as soon have let them run free.

A Focus on God

One day she and a friend were talking about the incident. "I wonder why it's so easy for a cat to catch mice," the friend said.

Many cats are extremely good hunters. Some people worry that if a cat comes into a neighborhood, it will wipe out all the birds. Yet naturalists who study these things find that wherever there are cats, there are more birds than in places where there are no cats.

It's as if nature requires a balance, and so nature provides.

As I put out seed for the sparrows in our backyard, I sometimes look around and think, *They're all over the place!* But then I notice that there are only as many sparrows as there is food to go around.

Recently I read that when the first bird finds food, it sends a call to others of its kind. If there is a lot of food, it sends a loud message, "Chow's on." And all the other birds come flying in.

But if there isn't enough to go around, it doesn't send out the call as loudly or clearly. This way, fewer birds will fly in to eat the food.

So the two friends were talking about the cat and how it is able to catch mice so easily. "If you watch a cat stalk a mouse," the ECKist said, "you notice that every fiber of its being is focused on the hunt. If we could only focus that intensely on something, just think what we could accomplish — especially if our focus was on God."

The ECKist had been wondering how to get further along in her spiritual life. She found it interesting that out of her own mouth came the words, "Focus on God the way a cat focuses on the hunt."

Mouse Watching

Several years ago we had a cat who tried to be a mouser, but he just wasn't very good at it.

One day he sensed something in the brush. He ran across the lawn to the edge of the brush and stuck his head in, watching for the mouse that apparently was a few feet farther in.

The cat was so excited that he started to swing his tail about in the dried grass. He made such a commotion that the mouse, forewarned that there was something big out there, quickly fled the scene.

Like I said, the cat wasn't a very good mouser, or a good example of how to focus on God.

Yet some people are just like that cat. They stick their nose into the hunting ground a little bit, thrash their tail around and make a big noise, then wonder why they don't get any results. They run from one spiritual path to another, making a lot of noise about how much they know about God.

The Tiger's Fang by Paul Twitchell includes a story about a man who was always bragging about his talks with God.

God doesn't come to people who make a big show of their own importance, which is why they have to make up stories about how close they are with God.

Just One Step Away

There are walls in this world. Sometimes God or a better life is so close, so close. But many people choose to stay on one side of the wall simply because they cannot recognize that a better life is right there on the other side.

A woman who worked in a doctor's office hated her job. The doctor was abusive to her, constantly scolding and criticizing her for everything she did.

Finally unwilling to take it anymore, she quit. *No matter how bad it is out in the world,* she thought, *I'll be better off than working for this doctor.*

Right after that she had an accident and broke her jaw. Unable to work and with large medical bills, her debts began to pile up. She decided to increase her future job prospects by going to nursing school. The added expenses put her so far in debt that she didn't know how she would ever get out from underneath her problems.

One day she got a call from a doctor who asked her to work in his office while his regular employee was out on maternity leave.

She took the job, and in a short time she found herself thinking, *This place is heaven!*

Oddly enough, it was in the same medical building where she had worked before. On the other side of the wall she could hear noises from the people who worked in the office of the doctor who had treated her unkindly.

"All that time," she said, "I was one footstep from heaven."

After all that trial and tribulation, she ended up back in the very same building. But this time she landed on the other side of the wall.

Change of Consciousness

Sometimes it's like this in your spiritual life. When things are going hard for you, you may wonder, *What's happening here? Has the Mahanta, the Inner Master, forgotten me? Has the Mahanta left me?*

Sometimes you need the experience of leaving something, of having the will to say, "This is not the way I want to live the rest of my life. I would like to do something else."

Once you decide to act on it, you find out that there are a lot of other things that come with a decision like this. Change means going from one state of consciousness to another. And this involves adjustments, which in most cases mean trouble. Adjustments equal trouble.

But when you get to the other side, all of a sudden you realize that things are better. That this life, this state, this new condition existed alongside the original one all along.

What, then, kept you from being there? The lack of courage to make a move, to do something.

Key to Happiness

People who work at the same company have different experiences. Some are entirely happy with the way they are treated by their superiors. Others, although treated the same way, are miserable. The same conditions are one person's heaven and the other person's hell.

What makes the difference? Is it the working conditions?

The circumstances in our everyday lives are nothing like the harsh abuses of war, yet there are conditions that aggravate us, that make us wonder what this life is all about. The simplest way to deal with this is to put your focus on God by doing the Spiritual Exercises of ECK. You may find yourself transported from your hell to the heaven that exists just one step away.

Whether a person is in ECK or not, it's their state of consciousness that makes them happy or unhappy.

It's what you do with what you have that makes all the difference. Whenever something comes into my life, I try to get the most out of it that I can.

A Way to Renew Yourself

There is a lot of attention on ecology nowadays. The Europeans are ahead of the Americans in garbage disposal habits because they have limited room for waste storage—landfills and so on. Separating the garbage into different categories has become a way of life.

If you tried to introduce a project like that here in the

States, there would be a long, slow period of reeducation as to how to go about it. And many people would protest, feeling that it was taking away their freedom.

In South America and the Middle East, archeologists have uncovered ancient cities that were abandoned suddenly. Scientists couldn't figure out why anyone would walk away from a perfectly good city. But as they dug through the rubble, they found that garbage had been thrown over the city walls until it was piled to the top of the walls. In time, the rats probably took up residence in the garbage and spread cholera and other diseases that threatened to wipe out the population, so everybody had to leave. Or maybe the garbage got so high that their enemies were able to climb up the pile and come over the wall.

Again, we have our castles, our walled cities around us. Why? Because the walls provide protection from the harsher things in life.

But as you go through life, you keep throwing off karma, those graceless little acts that accumulate like piles of garbage. You throw it over the wall.

Pretty soon, unless you figure out a good way to get rid of this waste, spiritual corruption sets in.

And so in ECK you need to do the Spiritual Exercises of ECK to continually renew yourself. These spiritual exercises help you to sort these things into little piles, some to be recycled and reused to help you along in your search for God.

Finding a Use

The nondiscriminating mind takes all the waste and throws it into one big heap. It's all waste; therefore it's all no good.

But the person who is further along on the spiritual path sorts through the waste before it gets to that great big pile and says, "Oh, this can be used by somebody else." They save the paper, save the clothing. And in so doing, they are giving back to life.

Years ago, when my daughter was three—an age when children make the most interesting remarks—she said, "Someday we're going to have to pay for the water we drink." These days, lack of water has become a crisis in some areas. Either there isn't enough to go around or the water is polluted. Yet, people continue to pollute it and think that life is always going to be fair and wonderful for them anyway.

It doesn't happen that way.

One of the most spiritually healthy programs to occur in recent years is the ecology movement. There are abuses, of course. Some of the people involved in the issue get quite fanatic about it. They don't use common sense.

They try to force everybody else to do it their way, without allowing time for society to make its changes naturally. In the interest of saving nature, they become very abusive to others. They don't see it that way, of course, piously feeling that they are doing this for a good cause.

Religious missionaries, too, often feel strongly that they are acting for a good cause.

In the past, they traveled to other countries and forced the natives to change their lifestyle and beliefs to suit the consciousness of the missionaries. Many atrocities were committed in the name of religion. It happened here too, when the Spaniards first came to the New World and brought Catholicism. They destroyed the records and libraries of the ancient Native Americans, considering them pagan works.

This is the vanity of people who think they have the last word on God.

The problem is not in what they think, it's in what they do. The torture, killing, or harassment of others who do not share the same beliefs that you do is a crime. Some might call it a sin; in ECK we say this is causing some heavy karma.

Law Student's Vacation

A young couple who live in Washington, D.C., were trying to figure out what to do about the husband's future. Should he pursue a legal education or what? They couldn't decide.

The wife, who was helping her husband through college and hoped he would go on to graduate school, made a suggestion. "While we're on vacation in Boston," she said, "why don't we look for symbols that might help us decide what you should do?"

They stopped to visit a small museum in Concord, Massachusetts. As they were about to pay the admission, the wife suddenly thought of a way they could save some money. "You're a student, remember?"

"Yeah, right," he said. "I can show them my student card and get a discount."

He showed his card to the person who collected admission fees. "Oh, you're from Georgetown University. Two other people are here from Georgetown right now." The husband scanned the guest register and recognized one of the names. They quickly went inside to greet his acquaintance, a professor of constitutional law. She had been one of his favorite teachers because of her ability to inspire him. The couple learned that she and another professor had just flown in from England the day before.

The wife marveled at the fact that the professors had chosen that day to travel to this little town in Massachusetts, far away from Georgetown University.

"You know, this was a waking dream from the ECK," she told her husband. "What are the chances that we four, who come from different directions, would bump into each other in this little museum in a small town in Massachusetts? I think it's simply because we asked the ECK for a sign about your future."

The husband agreed. This had to be a sign that he should continue with his education in law.

Learning to See and Listen

The ECK works in subtle ways. If there is something you need to know, you have to be of a mind to ask. Then you need the consciousness or awareness to know how the Holy Spirit speaks to you.

But so many people can't hear. Even in ECK, you first have to learn how to listen and how to see. You learn to listen for the Voice of God in whatever way It comes, and also to see the manifestation of the Light of God in whatever way It comes. The Holy Spirit, which is the Voice of God, is always working on your behalf to help you unfold spiritually, to become a better, more loving human being.

All that prevents you from taking that step is your state of awareness, your focus on God. How strong is it? How much do you want God?

How successful you will be depends on your answer.

I get so many wonderful letters from the members of ECK in Africa. They are naturally open to Divine Spirit. Their developing nations often are in turmoil, just as the

61

United States once went through its turmoils. People are more open to life when everything is up in the air and they constantly have to think on their feet.

Let Me See Your Pass

A Nigerian, entering the building where he worked, was stopped at the door by a security guard. "Do you work here?" the guard said, his tone challenging.

"Yes, I do," the ECKist said.

"May I see your pass?"

The ECKist opened his wallet and fished around for it. He finally found it and showed it to the guard. The guard was satisfied.

"You thought I was lying, didn't you?" the ECKist asked as he put his wallet back in his pocket.

"No," the guard said, "it's just that you have such a beautiful light on your face." He had detained him because he wanted to talk with him. You see, before the ECKist went to work that morning, he had done his contemplation as usual.

In contemplation you simply sit and quietly sing HU or some other holy name of God, allowing the Voice of God to come into you, either as love or as Light or Sound. Because the man had taken the time to contemplate, the Light of God had come into his heart and now shone in his face.

The guard saw this and was uplifted too.

It's a pleasure to be around someone who's shining with the Light of God. People who aren't in ECK don't always understand what's going on. All they know is that they are drawn to this person.

There is something special about him or her.

Light of God

The same ECKist reflected on a time when a relative, who wasn't a member of ECK, had visited his home. The ECKist was in his room in contemplation early one morning when the guest, not realizing his host was in there, happened to walk in. The ECKist heard the door open and then quickly close.

He finished his contemplation and left his room. "Excuse me," the guest said. "I didn't mean to bother you. I didn't know you were in there. But if I may ask, what were you doing? It looked like you were just sitting in the chair with this beautiful light coming from your face."

"That is the Light of God," the ECKist explained.

He then told the relative how he too could find this very same Light of God for himself and let it come into his heart.

The way to do this is to sing HU. I repeat this for those who are not used to the ways of Divine Spirit as we know It. They are used to the ways of Spirit as they know It, and this is why they are here.

There's No Hurry in ECK

Whenever you give a talk on ECK, you must understand that the people who come are there because of some inner connection beforehand.

The Mahanta or one of the other ECK Masters has been teaching them about the Light and Sound of God on the inner planes. Usually the people who attend your talks on ECKANKAR are not aware of what's going on inside. Nor are they aware that more than likely they were followers of ECK in another lifetime, but that they left the path because they had gone as far as they could in that lifetime.

You see, there's no hurry in ECK. People who have been at a certain initiation level for a while sometimes hint, "Well, I have pretty much learned everything there is to know as a Second Initiate." Broad hint. They don't realize that there is so much more to learn on that plane. And so I just acknowledge their hint inwardly.

They do not yet know that you don't go after God in the same way that you go after a promotion in the office. It's much different.

Secret Teachings

Another ECKist from Africa, an electrical engineer, went to the home of a retired school principal to do some electrical work. Although the retired principal was up in years, he told the ECKist he shared his house with his father.

As they worked on the wiring together, the ECKist was telling him about ECK when a very old man came into the room.

"Hey, what are you doing there, telling the secrets of ECK to this child?" said the old man. The child, of course, was the old man's son, the retired principal.

"They are not secret anymore," the ECKist said. "A man named Paul Twitchell brought them out to the public in 1965."

The old man thought about this for a while. Then he said, "I first heard about ECKANKAR in 1914." He described the ECK Master who had taken him to a Temple of Golden Wisdom in the inner worlds, the inner heavens. "He spoke to me about ECKANKAR. I see this teaching has finally made it out to the earth plane."

"What did this Master look like?" the ECKist asked.

"He had long blond hair," the old man said.

"I think I know who you met. I'll bring you a picture." The ECKist went home and found a picture of Gopal Das, an ECK Master who once served as the Mahanta, the Living ECK Master—the position that I fulfill today as the spiritual leader of ECKANKAR. He brought the picture to the old gentleman, who recognized the face immediately.

"Yes," the old man said, "that is the man who first told me about the teachings of ECK in 1914."

I like to mention these stories for the benefit of those who question how an organization founded in 1965 could be based on an ancient teaching. They may or may not accept it; they may or may not become members of ECK. Doubts can set in even after one steps on the path of ECK. At some point the person may begin to wonder, *Is the path of ECK really true? Is it really a teaching that has come to earth from the inner planes?*

So whenever these stories come to me, I share them. They come from people who have nothing to gain by telling of their previous association with ECKANKAR, often years before Paul Twitchell brought the teachings out again in 1965.

The Locksmith

One Friday night, an ECKist who was in charge of the local ECK Center was getting ready to close up and go home. The center, which was located in an office building, had several outer rooms and one inner room. She turned the lock on the door to the inner room and pulled it shut as she left. Out in the general area, she grabbed her purse and reached for her car keys, then suddenly realized she had locked them, along with her other keys, in the inner room.

What am I going to do now? she wondered. She called another ECKist who lived nearby.

"I've locked my keys in the inner room," she explained. "Could you bring your keys and open the door?"

Her friend came right over and tried to unlock the door with both of his keys. Neither one would open the inner door.

The two ECKists stood outside the door and wondered how to get her keys so she could go home. "We could break a window," he said.

"No, too messy," she said. "Let's break down the door."

"That could get pretty expensive," he cautioned. "Let's try to open it with my credit card. I saw it done in the movies. You just slip the card between the door and the jamb and work the bolt out of the lock. That should do the trick."

Well, they tried it, but the credit card was too stiff. It wouldn't go around that tight corner.

They went in search of the custodian. "Would you let us into the inner room in the ECK Center?" they asked.

"Sorry, I can't help you," he said. "I just have the keys to the building, not to any of the inner rooms."

Back in the ECK Center, one of them finally came up with the obvious solution. "Why don't we call a locksmith?" They looked in the yellow pages and found a locksmith who was on call twenty-four hours a day. He arrived in no time at all.

Putting his large assortment of tools on the floor, the locksmith got to work. When the first few tools failed to open the lock, he reached in his pocket, took out his wallet, and pulled out a credit card. The ECKists watched in amazement as he slipped his card between the door and the jamb and quickly opened the lock. The woman got her keys and went home.

Later, as she thought all this over, she said, "The inner door unlocks the secrets of the heart. Locked, it locks out the love of God. It has the keys to the car that I can use to go home—to God."

Why Do You Need a Master?

When the two ECKists used their mental resources to figure out how to get in the door, all they came up with were crude, messy ways, like breaking the window or the door. When they looked for help from the custodian, who represented Kal, the ruler of the lower worlds, he said, "No, I just have the keys for the outer doors"—the earth plane. He couldn't help them with the inner door. They tried a credit card, but it was too stiff; it wouldn't bend or give.

Finally they called on the locksmith who, like the Mahanta, was available twenty-four hours a day.

Instead of opening the door with the usual tools, he used his credit card. He used the same thing that they had. The only difference was, his was more flexible.

Why do you need a Master? Because sometimes he uses the talents you have, but he shows you in a more flexible way how to use your talents yourself. The difference between the Mahanta in ECKANKAR and a savior of another religion is this: A savior tries to save you from yourself; the Mahanta tries to help you to help yourself.

That is the basic difference.

The newly-released *ECKANKAR Journal* contains

beautiful stories of the kind I have mentioned this weekend, but often told much better. This is one of the best ways to answer people who ask you about ECK. Just say, "Here's an *ECKANKAR Journal.* My compliments. Read it, and if you have any more questions, we can talk later."

This can be very helpful to others. They will look at it and see that ECKANKAR and the teachings of ECK are very much alive in the daily life of the people on this most holy, spiritual path to God.

ECK Worldwide Seminar, Minneapolis, Minnesota,
Sunday, October 24, 1992

Suddenly I got the same feeling: *I've done this before.
And not just the other day but a long time ago.* A vague
memory of an old dream came back to me.

5

Is Life a Random Walk?

The first time I came to Australia was in 1981, and I've been back many times since. There is a freshness of spirit here.

The United States and Australia are both children of England. The States being the older child, we have lost some of the freedom. Younger children have more freedom in that they seem to take life more on its own terms. When you get older, you start to put conditions on life and what you want from it. Of course, if you put down too many conditions and rules that don't coincide with the rules of life, things go harder for you.

Changing Vision

I have been working with an optometrist for a number of months, hoping he'll come up with contact lenses that I can see with. I'm getting to that stage of life where my eyes don't accommodate as well as they did when I was younger. Like many of you, I've reached the bifocal age. I've been resisting it, of course.

"Hey, it happens to everybody," he tells me. "I know

that," I say. "But that doesn't mean it has to happen to me, does it?"

It's too bad that many people go through the stages of life so concerned with troubles that they don't notice the good times. This is something we begin to recognize as we get older.

Facing Life

Today I talked with a young lady of nineteen, the same age as my daughter. She had some of the same attitudes as my daughter, which basically amount to a great uncertainty about the future.

I can understand this. Those of us in the bifocal age and beyond sometimes forget the uncertainties we experienced when we were young. Now that we have found a way to make a living, found a mate, had a family, made payments on a home, and all those things, we forget that young people just coming out of school have to face this big, gray wall called life. It's intimidating; they don't know if they will ever get over that wall. But, of course, we all do.

You don't attack the wall, you just kind of walk up to it. As you get closer, you find that the wall recedes and changes shape and texture. Pretty soon the wall turns into something else—your first home, your family growing, and all the things that enrich your life.

Many times throughout the whole experience, and usually when things are difficult, you ask yourself, *What is this all about? Why am I here?* I never wondered about the meaning of life when times were good, only when they were bad. This is human nature.

When times are good, we're so busy enjoying life that we can forget there has to be a meaning to it. It's only when times are bad that we begin to wonder about the reason for it all.

Some people who approach the spiritual are skeptics. Being more enamored of scientific fact, they may not have a connection with the inner life. This isn't always true, of course. Some scientists today have a closer connection with the divine aspect of life than many clergymen who supposedly are leading people to God.

Is Life a Random Walk?

Is life a random walk or not? *Random walk* is a term known in the investment field. It affects people who try to make a living in financial markets by studying charts.

One day the trend may indicate that they should invest in the market now. A few days later the updated charts may tell them to sell and get out. Sometimes, no matter how diligently they study their charts, they suffer losses.

This is when they wonder, *Do these charts work, or is life a random walk? Is everything in life just a great big spin of the wheel of fortune? Is it all chance?*

Connecting the Inner and Outer Worlds

Last year we were in a restaurant. There were stairs leading to other businesses on the second floor. The place seemed vaguely familiar. Later we decided to go up the steps.

I noticed the brass railing as we walked up, and when we were almost at the top, I suddenly had the feeling that I had been there before. To the left there was a white door, shut and locked. I walked past and didn't think much of it.

Two days later we went back to the restaurant, but by then I had forgotten about the feeling I'd had the last time we were there. Again, we went up the stairs, and as I reached the third step from the top, suddenly I got the same feeling: *I've done this before. And not just the other day but a long time ago.* A vague memory of an old dream came back to me.

We returned to the restaurant a third time, and as we went up the stairs, I noticed that the door to the left was open. It was a private office. You wouldn't just walk into the office if you didn't have any business there. But with every step, I became more curious to see what was inside the room.

Looking through the doorway, I saw that it was a computer room. The walls and floor were all white. All around were computers, monitors, printers, and other machines.

The setup looked very commonplace to me except that I suddenly remembered the rest of the dream.

I'd had it back in the 1960s, when I first came into ECKANKAR. At the time it was a recurring dream, so real that I woke up very upset each time it came. I couldn't understand what I was seeing.

In the dream, somebody opened a white door and I walked into a small, roundish-shaped room. Everything was crisp and clean. There were numerous monitors that looked like television sets but smaller, and I knew there was something different about them. In front of each monitor was a keyboard, and nearby was a large printer. This was several years before computers, video monitors, and printers were everywhere. Because I couldn't relate it to anything I had seen on earth, I figured the dream must have been about a spaceship.

The computers and monitors in the dream room were

humming, and the printer made a muffled, clattering sound. "What are all these strange noises?" I said. You hear it all the time now, but back then I had never heard machinery make those particular sounds before. It felt all wrong.

The experience last year demonstrated once again that life is more than a random walk. There is something that connects the invisible worlds to the visible worlds.

Key to Inner Worlds

Most people, like myself at one time, are unaware that there is something beyond our everyday life, beyond this physical universe. They finish work, go home, have their evening meal, spend time with the family, and go to bed. Then they go totally blank until they wake up the next morning and begin another day in the physical world, with no remembrance of what took place the night before. People go through their life living half of it.

If you are not aware of what is happening to you in the dream state, in the invisible spiritual worlds, you are not living your life fully out here in the physical world. If you have never made a connection between your dream worlds and the world out here, you never will realize how much you're missing.

The Spiritual Exercises of ECK are the key to these inner worlds. They are the key to your secret worlds.

The Spiritual Exercises of ECK are simple. For example, in one all you do is close your eyes, at home or in some quiet place, and sing HU to yourself.

When you do the Spiritual Exercises of ECK, you set aside a time to be quiet and to open yourself to the Holy Spirit, which we call the ECK. This is very important. Because as you open yourself by singing HU, you are opening yourself to the opportunity to see and live your life better.

Harmony

The word *HU* will spiritualize you. It's an old name for God. Sing HU on the way to work, for instance, and you will find that you have a different way of looking at the people around you and at the work you do.

When you run into a problem, such as making a mistake that might cost the company money, sing HU to yourself. When you sing it you are saying, "I want to come into harmony with life. Quite obviously I'm out of it at this moment, or I wouldn't have made this mistake."

Someone might approach you in anger, and suddenly the area around you is thrown out of harmony. You may feel that you have to holler back, and sometimes you do, but there is another way.

Rather than respond with anger, sometimes it's better just to quietly chant HU and listen to the other person.

A Gift from the Master

There are people who expect anyone who says he is a spiritual leader to write down the rules. They figure they can take the book home, read it, and become very spiritual too. To them I would say, "Well, OK, here are the rules, and good luck."

What people do not understand is that you cannot find God or a high state of consciousness or truth by reading a book.

I have to be quite honest and say that you are not going to find God by listening to me or anyone else give a talk. I can inspire you and give you knowledge—I can do those things. But even when I hand you specific knowledge, such as, "Sing HU when you're in trouble or in need," you may not accept the gift.

Yet this is what I can do for you, and you might as well know that right from the beginning. The rest of the time I'm going to encourage you to look to the inner side of the ECK teachings.

In ECK we recognize the principle of the Inner and the Outer Master. I can be there on the inner side when you cry, when you have no one to listen to you, and also in times of joy, when there is no one to share your joy with you.

Basically, I can only give you HU. But precious though it may be, the gift is nothing unless you do something with it yourself.

Beyond the Mind

Any rule book I could write about the laws of God can help you, but if all you do is read it, then the most it will do is help you to mentalize the principles of the Holy Spirit. Very mental people will not get to God, because the mind cannot go to God. It's that simple.

The mind is a creation of the material worlds of matter, energy, space and time. As you rise in consciousness, there is a point at which the mind must stay; it does not go past a certain level.

It is as Soul, the spiritual being, a spark of God, that you go beyond the mind, into the higher worlds of God.

I'm speaking now of worlds beyond the lower heavens, beyond the Astral, Causal, Mental and Etheric Planes. The higher worlds start in the Soul Plane and go on into the heart of God. At that level there is only the Light and Sound of God. Sometimes the Light is very, very bright.

Twin Aspects of the Holy Spirit

There is so much information out in the public today about near-death experiences. You've read about them, you've seen reports on TV and in the movies. Twenty-five or thirty years ago, you didn't dare tell anyone about these things, but now it's almost commonplace.

Many people have spoken about their experiences while on the brink of death, and one of the things described most often is the white light. Others have experienced the sound of a choir or of someone speaking to them. This is all part of the Light and Sound of God.

The Light of God is seen in so many ways. Sometimes It's white, sometimes bluish, sometimes pinkish or yellow. Some see It as a globe, a torch, or a flashlight. It may appear as a little speck of light, blinking like a star, or as a very beautiful sparkling blue light shaped like a star. All these different shades and shapes are of the Light and Sound of God, which are the two aspects of the Holy Spirit.

Understanding about Love

In Christianity I think there is a great misunderstanding about the Holy Spirit. It is conceived of as a being, one of the three persons of the trinity.

But It is not a person; It is Spirit in the true sense. It is not something that we can put into words any more than we can say God is this or God is that. Trying to put it into human terms, we may say, "God is love." But this is not the full definition of God either.

Ask any person to demonstrate love in his daily life. Watch how he deals with others, at home and at work.

Many times you might conclude that he or she is a very poor example of a Christian or an ECKist or whatever.

Why? Because the attitude you'll see demonstrates all this individual knows about the quality of love.

If they know how to be kind and gentle to themselves but are mean-spirited and angry with others, how much understanding does this person have about love? This leads to another question: How much understanding can a person like that have of God?

Do you see my point? So many people claim to know all about God, but a look at how they conduct themselves in their daily life says it isn't so.

We will never be able to define God with the human faculties. The most you can do—and this is all that I hold out for you—is to experience a state, a God state. This is the experience of God-Realization. It may not mean anything to you at this time, and I don't expect it to, but it gives you the ability to experience happiness and joy out here. Sometimes, for no reason at all, you suddenly feel so happy that you could sing.

Forty Trainees

There once was a master tradesman who had always worked by himself. One day he realized that he was getting along in years. "I think it's time to get some people together to help me," he said. "I'm going to find forty trainees. If I teach each one of them all the rules of this trade, they will be able to duplicate me forty times over."

The man went out to look for trainees. During the next five years he handpicked forty people from all walks of life. Some were well educated, others were not; some were rich, others poor; some were ambitious while others couldn't have cared less about success.

The man was curious. What would happen? While this was a good way to use his knowledge to expand his

79

business, he was also a student of human nature. And this was an experiment.

Each of the forty trainees were given the rules of the trade. The master tradesman wrote them down step-by-step, making them as simple as he could. He supervised each person individually. Long hours were spent each day in an effort to give the students his very best knowledge.

The master invested the same amount of time with each of the trainees. Five years later, he gave up the experiment and sent his pupils out into the world. The result: Only five out of the forty became successful in that particular trade.

What happened? Why were they not each a success? The answer, quite simply, is human nature.

Some of the trainees were so egotistical about their educational backgrounds that they came in thinking they already knew everything. When the boss said, "Use this particular rule," the trainees thought, *No, I know better than that. This rule won't work.* Others were just plain lazy. When the teacher said, "This is what you should do as you make your plans to move a little further ahead," these people would shortcut the sequence of rules he laid out for them.

Some of the trainees didn't have the patience, others tried hard but just were not flexible enough in life to make the necessary quick moves back and forth. Some were too rigid in their thinking, some were too deep in their thinking, and others didn't delve deeply enough.

A Passion for What You Do

Most of the trainees failed because they didn't have the same passion as the master for what he had accomplished. And without the passion, they didn't have the self-discipline.

Each trainee was given the rules. They had the master standing right over their shoulder, guiding them for five years. But lacking the passion for what they were doing, they didn't have the love for it. Passion, self-discipline, and love go together. In any sport, hobby, talent, or job that you really enjoy, you will spend whatever time it takes to improve and refine your skills.

People who do not share your love for this endeavor will either admire your drive or say you're crazy to put so much effort into something they think is pointless. How many times have you heard that? When you really want to do something well, there will always be people around you who are all too ready to discourage you. "Hey, you're working too hard!" they'll say. They can't understand why the task isn't the same drudgery and pain for you as it is for them.

For you it's joy, for you are doing something you love.

And because you love it, you gain strength and energy in doing it. This energy and love in you will attract other people with the same feelings. It's the old story of birds of a feather flocking together.

Vain Perspectives

The idea of finding truth is similar no matter what religion you are in, because all religions are of God. If more people understood this, they wouldn't be so eager to tear other religions apart.

Some religions are based on the negative power, of course, such as those that get into the sacrifice of other human beings. Nevertheless, all too often we like to think that our religion is of God while all the others are of the negative power. This wouldn't be something called vanity, would it?

It's human nature to think that whatever we know, whatever we follow is the BEST, in capital letters. And whatever anybody else follows, well, they'll be lucky to get out of this world alive.

If we can laugh at ourselves and laugh *with* others instead of at them, the laughter itself is the music of God. Sometimes this is the first music we come across. It's a matter of finding joy in life.

"I Want to Go Home"

A child was born with a valve in her stomach that didn't work properly. The doctors had no idea whether or not she would outgrow this condition. Throughout her childhood, her parents would introduce her to strangers by saying, "This is our daughter. She was born with a defect in her stomach, and she can't keep food down very well." This added an extra burden to this poor child's youth.

One day when she was very young, the problem turned into a crisis. Her parents found her turning blue, and she was rushed to the hospital. Luckily she pulled through. The doctors who treated her thought she would be all right now.

The child had an older sister who always made fun of her. Soon after she came home from the hospital, the older sister picked a fight with her.

As I was growing up, my older brother was at the top of the totem pole. I was second. If I did something that made him unhappy, he'd pound on my arm. We learned early that we couldn't pound each other in the face because our parents wouldn't stand for bloody noses or broken bones. But my brother discovered that if he pounded me on the arm, he could do as much damage as possible and it wouldn't show. This is similar to what happened to the young girl. Her older sister wasn't allowed to beat her up physically, but she figured she could get away with verbal abuse and name-calling.

On that particular day, the younger girl got tired of it and beat up her older sister, who ran and told their father. He angrily sent the little girl to her room. She had just recovered from a serious condition, her sister had started the fight, and she's the one who got sent to her room. She lay on her bed, thinking about the injustice.

"I want to go home," she cried. "I just want to go home." In a spiritual sense she was saying, "I want to go home to God because I'm so unhappy here."

This is in line with the concept that God is someplace else, or that Soul is estranged from God. True, each of us on this earth plane is Soul, and at one time Soul lived in the highest heavens of Light and Sound. Without the discipline to serve others, Soul served Itself. God sent Soul into the lower worlds so It could get the experience needed to learn the nature of love. This is why you are here, and the first lesson of life is to learn to love yourself.

When the little girl on the bed cried, "I want to go home, I just want to go home," she was speaking in the spiritual sense, as Soul. In her misery, she was remembering unconsciously that she really didn't belong here on earth, that she was just a traveler here, a visitor.

Accepting Life for What It Is

But as the girl heard her own words, she suddenly snapped out of it and came back to earth, away from the remembrance of Soul in the bliss of God. *I am home,* she realized.

She didn't mean the heavenly home this time. Now she was thinking in physical terms. "I'm as home as I'm going to get," she said, "and it isn't going to get better. So I might as well put up with it until I'm old enough to leave." She stopped crying then, because she had come to an important realization: Things might not get better, but actually they were pretty good right where she was.

All she had to do was to accept life as it was right then. This was a pretty important realization for such a young person.

How to Accomplish a Dream

Many people much older don't understand that. They continue to live out there somewhere, far beyond arm's reach. There's nothing wrong with it. But sometimes their dreams are so far beyond their reach that they don't even try to attain them, they just spend their days dreaming and wishing. While doing that, they don't reach even the simplest goals that might make life better for them.

The way to accomplish a dream is to take the first step. If I want to go through the doorway over there, I can dream all I want, but until I take the first step, I'm never going to get there.

Then, once I take the first step, I have to take the second, third, and so on. If I persist, eventually I will get to the doorway.

The same applies to the doorway of truth. You can dream of heaven, of God, and of truth all you like. But unless you take the first step, you'll never get there. And the first step I'm giving you is the word *HU.* Sing it to yourself, out loud when you're alone or silently when other people are around.

Hand of God

The girl grew up, got married, and went through many hardships. She lost her firstborn son, and her marriage almost went to pieces. There were other tragedies too numerous to mention.

One day she was sitting in church—she was a Catholic. Depressed and despondent, she felt that she had hit rock bottom. There was a prayer service going on, and people were seated all around her, praying. All of a sudden, in the depths of her despair, she felt a hand on her shoulder. She opened her eyes quickly and turned around to see who it was. There was no one near her.

In a way, you can say that this was the hand of God, sent through the hand of one of God's messengers. God ITSELF—in ECK we don't say Him or Her—does not come down into the human theater and walk among the people of the world in the sense that we normally would like to believe.

But there are spiritual beings sent as messengers from God, perceived as angels and that sort of thing. The woman realized that her guardian angel had placed a hand upon her shoulder.

Two Streams

Though I said a hand rather than his or her hand, you'll notice that I also did not say its hand. The people in the other worlds are not asexual; they are not without sex.

These messengers, the angels and so on, usually are men or women. The lower worlds, which include all the heavens up to the Soul Plane, are worlds of duality; everything exists by and because of its opposite, male and female. These lower worlds, even those far beyond the Astral and Causal Planes, are still fed through the divine action of the Holy Spirit, the Light and Sound. Light and Sound in the high worlds are one action.

In the lower worlds there are two forces, very different, which we see as either the positive or the negative force. And in each person there are these two currents, stronger or weaker. This is not to say that men are the positive force and women the negative, or vice versa. It doesn't work that way.

You have both streams within you, and one of the streams, the positive or the negative, is stronger. This is how it is.

These streams are of the Light and Sound of God in each person. This is what makes the light of Soul. If the light of some Souls is very dim, it is because people are at different states of consciousness. They are at different spiritual levels, and so their lightbulbs shine with different brightnesses.

Eternity Here and Now

The woman in church recognized that something was going on. This was her assurance that life is more than a random walk. Somebody had touched her.

As a Catholic who was more grounded in the physical side of life than in the mystical, this realization was quite startling to her. But the years passed. In time she had another son. As he grew up, he became interested in spiritual things. The woman was too, but she was willing to wait.

Her approach to life was that when the student was

ready, the Master would appear. After all, she had already spent years waiting to find the next step to truth after feeling the hand on her shoulder. Her son, with the impatience of youth, took a different approach. "Eternity now," he would say. In ECK we say, spiritual freedom here and now.

One day the son was reading an ECK book, and in the back was a phone number. "What are you reading?" his mother asked.

"There's something in here about eternity here and now," he said. "I'm going to call this number and see what I can find out."

The voice on the other end of the line told him about an upcoming meeting where someone would explain more about the teachings of ECK. "I'm going," he told his mother. Though leery of any religious teaching other than the one she was used to, she decided to go with her son, just to make sure that nobody took advantage of him.

"Mother, please," he said, "don't make a scene." He could imagine his mother hurling angry accusations at the group. "If you promise not to embarrass me, you can come along."

The mother and son went to an introductory meeting on the teachings of ECK. At the end of the talk, the speaker said to the group, "To give you a better idea of what I'm talking about, I would like to invite you all to sing HU with me." Then, very softly, the speaker and all the others in the room began to chant HU.

The woman was reminded of a time three years earlier when she had gone to a renaissance fair where astrology and many other paths were represented.

In a little room where people came to meditate was a crystal bowl. Someone took a stick with a rubber tip, and as he ran the tip around the edge of the bowl, it made a wonderfully soothing sound. The woman found it beautiful and healing. In fact, when the renaissance fair returned the following year, she went back just to hear that special sound.

Now, two years later at an ECK meeting with her son, the woman sat there and listened to the others chant HU. *That sound, that sound,* she thought. Suddenly she realized that this was the soothing sound she'd heard at the fair.

The stick with the rubber tip running slowly around the crystal bowl had made the sound of HU, an ancient name for God.

When she found out that an audiocassette of a HU Song was available at the ECK meeting, she got so excited that she bought one. Her son was very surprised. "What are you doing, Mother? You never buy these things." She explained that it was the same wonderful sound that she'd heard at the renaissance fair and she wanted to hear it some more.

A Trip to the Temple

Mother and son became members of ECK, and soon after that, the Temple of ECK was built in Chanhassen, Minnesota, very near Minneapolis. "Let's drive to Minnesota and see this Temple," he said.

"Yes," she agreed. "Maybe we'll have a great experience there." She knew this. She felt it. It reminded her of when she was a child, sobbing on her bed, "I want to go home. I just want to go home." She didn't understand what she meant then, and she didn't understand what she meant now.

They left their home on the East Coast with a 1968 map of Minneapolis. So many changes had taken place since then. When they reached the outskirts of Chanhassen, they asked a young man at a gas station, "How do we get to the Temple of ECK?"

"Never heard of it," he said.

They got back in the car and decided to try to find the center of town. To make matters worse, it was getting dark, and they couldn't see very far.

They found their way to the center of the little town of Chanhassen, knowing that the Temple of ECK had to be nearby. Driving down the main street, the woman suddenly got a strong feeling of déjà vu. She braked to a stop right in the middle of the street.

"Mother!" her son said. "What's the matter?"

She was frozen at the wheel. "I've been here before," she said.

Some years ago she'd had a recurring dream of coming to a small town where it was always winter and always cold. Except for a brief spell we call summer, that would describe Minneapolis.

In her dream she would walk up and down the sidewalk, past the hardware store, and then she'd see the town clock. It was always the same. She would wake up with the feeling that the dream was more real than her waking life. She had forgotten all about the recurring dream until this particular night when she got lost trying to find her way to the Temple of ECK.

"I've been here before," she repeated. She started to tell her son about the dream, but the traffic behind her was backing up and she had to move along. "Let's go back out to the highway in this direction," she said.

"I see a light over there to the west, on the hill," her son said. "Let's try that first." They drove over there and found the Temple of ECK.

The Temple of ECK is a very special place. If you ever have a chance to visit, come and see it for yourself. I'm not saying it's special because it's our temple. The fact is, it's not our temple. You might say it's a temple for the world and we are just the caretakers. The Temple of ECK has its own presence, a very definite, good presence. It has the presence of the Light and Sound. Those of you who visit will notice something very special.

The Great Experience

They parked their car, went inside, and took seats. The woman waited quietly, wondering to herself, *When will I have my great experience?* As quickly as she asked, a soft voice came out of nowhere and said, "Well, what do you want? Do you need to get run over by a truck?"

Someone asked me today, "How do people in ECK usually find truth?" What he meant was, Does it come like a bombshell?

Well, it may be a dramatic experience, but often it's so subtle that when it does come, many people don't recognize it. This woman just had a marvelous experience where she physically found the place of her recurring dreams of years ago. Yet, just a few minutes later, she's sitting in the Temple of ECK waiting for a great experience.

The ECK Masters who are often there in the Soul body were probably saying, "Here's another one who doesn't show much promise. There's a good chance she'll go far on this path to God." You see, sometimes the people who start out as the greatest skeptics and doubters go the farthest on the path to God. So to those who would say, "Is there any hope for me? I don't buy any of this," all I would say is, "Fine. Nobody's selling."

I can give you truth. I can give you the word *HU*. I can show you techniques. But the factor that will make it work or not is your self-discipline. Are you going to spend time each day opening yourself to the Holy Spirit? Are you going to do it with love and with a passion? Are you going to put your whole mind and heart into this?

If so, you are going to make progress in life. You are going to find that the mysteries of today are no longer mysteries tomorrow.

Inner Sounds

After this woman came into ECK, she learned that the buzzing sound she had heard in the past is one of the manifestations of the Sound of God. A buzzing sound comes at a certain level we call the Etheric Plane. This is the area of the subconscious right before the Soul Plane— a high state of being.

Without knowing it, this is where the woman had left off in a previous life. For one reason or another, she didn't quite make it to the Soul Plane, but very early on in this life, she began to hear this buzzing sound.

Another sound she'd heard also began to make sense. It was the high, piercing note of a musical instrument. It doesn't hurt your ears, but it keeps going higher until it's beyond your hearing, lifting you upward spiritually. Again, this is the Voice of God speaking to you.

The Voice of God is the Holy Spirit in Its twin manifestations of Light and Sound. The highest of these two manifestations is always the Sound.

You hear a lot now about the light that some people have seen in near-death experiences. Because the Light is the lower of the two manifestations, more people will come across It. The higher manifestation is some form of the Sound. Sometimes It is heard as a choir singing, as a huge orchestra, as monks doing the Gregorian chant from medieval times, or in many other ways.

The Sound of God comes into your life to uplift you spiritually. Each sound corresponds to one of the planes of God, and that is where you are spiritually. Often it shows the level you reached in a previous lifetime.

In this lifetime, you are waking up again, coming to the spiritual path, taking the next step.

I would like to leave you tonight with the blessing of the Vairagi Masters. *Vairag* means detachment, not in a bad sense but in the sense of living above the emotions of the human plane, in the Light and Sound of God. The blessing is very simple: May the blessings be.

ECK South Pacific Regional Seminar, Sydney, Australia, Saturday, December 5, 1992

Just as the jade master pressed this green stone into the young man's hand, the Mahanta, the Inner Master, presses the spiritual exercise with the word *HU* to your heart every day.

6

The Jade Master

The title of this talk is "The Jade Master." I was going to call it "Grace and Truth," but who wants to listen to a talk on that? Most people would prefer to hear about something they don't know.

The theme in ECK this year is graceful living. Again, many people think they know as much about that as they need to. They would rather get on to the real truths in ECK.

Being Gracious Every Day

But one of the most important things we need to learn is how to be gracious and graceful in our everyday life. It's bad enough when a problem comes up, but then our reaction usually makes it worse.

For instance, if someone at work gets on our nerves, we rarely take the time to count to ten and try to respond gracefully. Instead, the other person barely gets the words out of his or her mouth, and we react. We become angry, fire back, defend ourselves—all these things. Before you know it, there's a full-scale war going on right there at work, with both sides feeling that they are in the right.

If two people come out of an argument feeling that they are in the right, you can be sure there are going to be sparks the next time they meet.

The only time there are not quite as many sparks is if the other person is in a higher position, such as the boss. Then you have to be careful how many sparks you throw back. After all, the economy is down.

The Rude Taxi Driver

There have been times I could have shown more grace. My wife and I had a stopover in England on our way back from Africa a few years ago. When we arrived at Heathrow, my wife was very tired and just wanted to get to the hotel and rest.

Outside was a long queue of taxicabs. We went to the front of the queue and asked the driver to take us to London. He didn't really want to do it. At that time of day, he informed us, it would be a one-way fare and he would have to make the long drive back for nothing. He'd rather wait for a more profitable local trip. He was very rude, and besides that, he was drunk.

When we wouldn't back down, the taxi driver finally said, "Just set your bags down and get in. I'll be there as soon as I'm finished with some business."

His business, it turned out, was gabbing with the drivers of the cabs lined up behind him. We sat there and waited.

When I'd had enough, I very ungraciously got out of the cab and opened the front door. Then I scooped our bags off the sidewalk and began throwing them onto the front seat. The driver saw me and came running over. "You can't do that," he said. "I do that."

"Well, why don't you do it then?" I said.

"I'll get to it. Get back in." I wasn't even in the cab for the count of ten before he went back to talk to his cronies.

I popped out of the taxi again, pulled open the front door, and threw all our bags down on the sidewalk. The driver came running back again. He didn't want our fare, but he didn't want to be embarrassed in front of his friends either.

"Are you a driver or not?" I asked.

"Yeah, I'm a driver," he said.

"Well, then, why don't you start driving?" These things seem pretty simple to me.

He just stood there looking upset for a minute, then got in the cab. A woman came over and introduced herself as the traffic director for the taxicabs. "What is the problem?" she asked.

I described the problem very briefly and said I wanted to take the next cab. She explained that in England you cannot take taxicab number two when cab number one is sitting there.

"The man is drunk," I said.

While we were talking, my wife got out of the cab and another passenger came out of the terminal and jumped in. The driver took off immediately.

"Well, I can't have him driving if he's drunk," said the traffic director, who was facing away from the queue of taxis.

"It's too late," I said. "There he goes."

"Would you like me to help you get a taxicab?" she asked. She was a very gracious woman who tried to be of help, and we certainly did not blame her.

"No, thank you," we said. "We'll just take the bus."

Learning Lessons

There are times you stew over a situation like this for weeks, imagining all the ways you could have played out the scene. Or you tell yourself that the circumstances made you act less gracefully than you could have. But then you say, "Well, so what."

In this case, I felt that the man had taken advantage of us. The rule was, if the passenger rejects the ride, the taxi driver can take the next person. He was just stalling with his friends, waiting for us to become impatient and quietly leave. I left, but I was anything but quiet.

There are other situations that cause impatience. A person who has traveled quite a distance just wants to get to the hotel, take a shower, and have some peace and quiet. But for some reason, this is when the normally efficient people at the check-in desk become totally incompetent. Soon you become angry and less graceful than you wish you had been. Later you say, "I wish I hadn't done that, but it was their fault."

Sometimes you rearrange things just so you can live with yourself. That's another definition of graceful.

Each of us is Soul, and we are here to learn lessons. One of the great lessons is to learn to love yourself, because until you can do that, you cannot learn to love someone else.

And until you can learn to love yourself and others, you cannot truly love God. Loving ourselves is hard for many of us to do because we know ourselves so well. But it's a necessary step, and we have to do the best we can.

Test of Grace

The travel agent who arranged our trip to the seminar assured us that we could stay on the same plane all the way to Sydney. We were so relieved that we wouldn't have to change planes, which usually means sitting around an airport for two hours or more.

We checked into the airport in Minneapolis and were assured once again, this time by the person at the ticket counter, that we could stay on the plane.

When we landed in San Francisco, the flight crew and most of the passengers got off, leaving just a few of us who were going on to the next leg of the trip. It was late at night and we were glad we could stay where we were and get some sleep.

Just as I got as comfortable as you can on an airplane, the supervisor of the flight attendants came into the cabin.

"The other flight crew hasn't arrived yet," he announced, "so I have to ask all of you to leave this plane."

You could tell he didn't want to be the bearer of this news; he was the type who didn't like to do unpleasant things. If you're a supervisor who doesn't like to do unpleasant things, you could easily lose the respect of your people. Taking the bad with the good is part of the job. But there's a right way and a wrong way—graceful or ungraceful—to go about it.

One test of a supervisor's grace is when confronting an employee who comes to work late. You can say, "The company pays us to start at a certain time and you've been coming in late. Would you like to talk about this? Is there a problem?" That's probably a graceful way to handle it. A less gracious way would be to call the employee into the office and explode: "What's the matter with you? Everybody else makes it in on time!" At that point the employee is probably thinking, *Yeah, aren't they foolish. And I'm supposed to be like the rest of them and come on time to a job I hate? That's crazy.*

So you have two people who are operating on entirely different sets of rules. Employee and supervisor are seated on opposite sides of the negotiation table but not talking the same language. The employee is probably unhappy with the working conditions or the pay, while the supervisor takes this approach: You have a good job, and I need you here to get the work out so I can pay you.

Back in the airplane, I was so tired. I didn't want to get off, even if he was the supervisor of every flight attendant in the world. I simply didn't care.

"The FAA says you have to get off," he said, noticing that we hadn't moved. The FAA, of course, is the regulatory agency that controls the U.S. airline industry. An ungraceful scenario began to play itself out in my mind. It went something like: "This is a real inconvenience, Jack. Do you know that? I'm not going to budge! If you want me off, you're going to have to carry me off! And I'm not going without my bags!" I pictured myself hanging on to the seats, screaming at him as he tried to pull me to the exit.

Outwardly I said, "That's fine. We'll get off." I was downright gracious as I gently explained that others had told us we wouldn't have to leave the plane until we got to Sydney. I waited politely for his response.

"The other flight crew hasn't come yet," he finally said.

"Well, where is the other flight crew?"

"I don't know."

"In that case," I said, "we will get off so that you can

clear the plane and do everything the right way."

"Oh, thank you so much," he said.

"You're welcome," we replied.

We left the plane and took our luggage with us; they don't guarantee its safety. As we passed the supervisor, he said, "You can preboard even before the first-class passengers."

"Thank you so much," we said.

He walked past us later in the terminal and smiled very nicely.

Then came the preboarding announcement, which was interesting in itself. The voice that spoke over the microphone said, "People who are preboarding may now board."

My wife and I started for the door. The ticket agent took our tickets, tore off the stubs, and said, "Wait, you can't go on yet."

The announcement blared out again over the microphone: "People who are preboarding may now board."

We moved ahead. "Stop," said the ticket agent.

"Go," came the announcement.

"Stop," he said. His job was to make it as hard as possible for the passengers to get on that plane.

Finally we were seated again. The supervisor came down the aisle and gave us a broad smile. "Oh, thank you," he said. "You're welcome," we answered, smiling back. *It's a good thing he didn't see the scene that had gone through my mind,* I thought.

Bringing Joy with You

This morning I was talking with a couple who live in a suburb of Sydney. The wife, a very happy, competent person, had taken a job in a company where there had been a lot of antagonism and anger going on before she started. She has been there for a year.

Shortly after she began, a coworker said to her, "Ever since you came here, things have been so much better. There's a lot of laughter and joy now. We never had that before."

The woman was so glad to hear that. She and her husband were going through particularly hard times then. He had lost his job, and they were struggling to raise a family with considerably less income. But rather than bring her problems to work, she would tell herself, "Things may be bad but I've got a job, and I might as well be happy with what I have." She carried her good attitude to work, and by doing this, she brought other people into this state of happiness and joy.

And someone noticed the joy she carried with her. Most people do not recognize it well enough to speak of it. So if you're looking for praise as you carry the Light of God that's in your heart to others, most often you're going to be unfulfilled.

Concept of Heaven

You serve as a Co-worker with God because of your love for God, not because someone else will notice. One of the essential precepts in ECK is that we are here on earth to learn love and compassion, to become a more perfect spiritual being. In so doing, both here and in the afterlife, we are then qualified to become Co-workers with God. So the concept of heaven in ECKANKAR is quite different from that in Christianity.

Many Christians believe that you make it to heaven only after a life filled with misery and tragedy. Life on earth is merely to be endured. They want to go to heaven because they think there will be a place prepared for them where, finally, they will be happy. And even if heaven did mean "a vacation for eternity," most don't really want to go, because you know the price of that.

I was mentioning to my wife that one of the things people on earth value so highly is the sex drive. Yet, this area of life is totally excluded from the Christian concept of heaven. "What a peculiar thing," I said.

"Well, if heaven is going to be that way," she said, "I suppose that's why they created purgatory. They needed a place for people who really would not want to go to heaven."

Spiritual Unfoldment Never Stops

In ECK, we do not expect a vacation for eternity after this life is over. What we expect is a steady progression in spiritual unfoldment from this life to the next life, and on and on. You do in the other life what you ought to be doing in this life: you serve life and give to others, sometimes in the humblest way. This is how you learn to become a Co-worker with God.

As you become a Co-worker with God, you are given more and more responsibilities. In other words, one day you rise in responsibility to become, in essence, a supervisor in the spiritual works. This applies both here and on the other planes. Some of those in supervisory roles are known as angels, elementals, and things like this, though, frankly, they are not very high up. There are other beings who actually run worlds and universes. This is their job.

Beings at all different levels work as Co-workers with God. They have proved themselves at the previous level, and now they have moved on to greater learning experiences.

Spiritual unfoldment never stops; it goes on and on. No matter how far you have come today, you can go further tomorrow. And no matter how far you come in this lifetime, of necessity you must go much further in your next lifetime. Spiritual law requires that you go either forward or backward.

This is a fact of life, a spiritual principle. You must unfold, or you shrink spiritually. Things move forward or backward.

Staying Flexible

This is why we have such wonderful teachings in ECK. At some point you no longer have to concern yourself with questions like What is this life all about? or What is the next life all about? Part of the process of unfolding spiritually is to learn what makes your life more interesting and better, and also the things to stay away from.

For instance, I used to enjoy eating a lot of fruit, but as I got older, I found it too acidic for my system. A couple years back, my hands got so stiff that I couldn't write.

So I went to a store and bought those little spongelike things that fit over pencils and make them bigger and easier to grasp. It reminded me of the huge pencils we used in our very early school days. I guess the teachers think little children can't handle regular pencils, so they give them logs.

Now I find that if I go easy on apples, oranges, grapefruit, and other fruits, my hands and joints stay flexible.

These are the some of the little things that you learn in your own life. Rather than complain about them, I'm grateful that I can identify the cause of problems that come up and try to resolve them.

But even at that, life sometimes has a way of bringing you problems faster than you can assimilate them. Other times, everything is going along fine, and then life makes a sudden change on you, such as an illness.

Was It Something I Ate?

Something that strikes me funny are the flu epidemics that go around periodically. I don't mean to sound heartless, but I have found that there is a close connection between major holidays and flu epidemics, which usually follow about two weeks later.

Of course, you don't dare suggest to people that they are ill because they have been eating like pigs. To keep the peace, I generally say something like, "Oh, could it be something you ate?"

"Oh, no, definitely not!" they insist, then proceed to cite the name of the latest popular flu strain they heard on the news. "It's certainly not the food I ate!"

"Well, then, certainly not," I say. It can turn into a less-than-graceful encounter if you push it.

In the United States, the flu virus intensifies after Thanksgiving, which comes at the end of November. You barely have time to clean out your system, then here comes Christmas and tons of foods that you just have to eat.

Many people buy a turkey so huge that the whole family couldn't finish it if they ate it every day for a week. Yet after each meal you put it back in the refrigerator, where it slowly deteriorates over the next several days. But since you paid a lot for the thing, you're going to eat it, and by the end of a week, the meat is pretty well spoiled. This can add to the flu too.

A lot of people haven't learned that in order to have food for the holidays, you don't have to buy a thirteen-pound turkey. You can buy something smaller, such as a Cornish hen, and if it makes you feel better, call it a turkey. This is the kind of thing they do on airplanes.

Truth or Fiction?

On our last trip, the flight attendant asked, "Would you like chicken or beef?"

"I'll try the chicken," I said.

A little while later she brought this tiny little thing on a plate. "They've served us pigeon again," I told my wife.

"Just eat your food," she said. "Don't play with it."

Truth is a funny thing. How do you get it? As I mentioned last night, I can speak of wisdom and truth and even put a whole list of rules in a book. There are people who feel they can gain in spiritual unfoldment merely by reading it at home. We can provide a lot of ECK reading material, sure; but without self-discipline and a strong desire and love for truth and for God, I can virtually guarantee that a person will not get very far in this lifetime.

The Jade Master

"The Jade Master" is a story in a book by Ed Seykota called *The Trader's Window.* It's about a young man who didn't know what to do with his life.

He had heard about a man known as the jade master who lived about five miles away. One day the young man said to himself, *Even though it's winter, I'm going to visit the jade master and learn all about jade.*

So he walks five miles through the snow and bitter cold. Finally he comes to the jade master's house and knocks on the door. An old man with a broom in his hand opens it. "Yes? What can I do for you?"

The young man says, "I've come to learn about jade. Would you take me as your student?"

"Sure," the old man says. "Come on in."

Inside the house the jade master makes the young man a cup of green tea, then presses a green stone into his hand. "Hold that while we talk," he says. And as they sip their tea on this cold winter day, the old man begins telling a story about a green tree frog.

The young man becomes very impatient. He doesn't want to hear about tree frogs. "Excuse me," he says, "I came here to learn about jade."

"Oh, excuse me," the old man says. "Why don't you come back next week?"

Puzzled, the young man heads for home. The following week he trudges all the way back through five miles of cold snow. The old man opens the door and lets him in. He makes the hot tea, presses this green stone into the student's hand, and again begins to talk about a green tree frog.

This time the young man is able to listen a little bit longer. Finally he says, "Excuse me, but I came here to learn about jade." He thinks the old man is going senile on him.

"Oh, excuse me," the jade master says. "Maybe you'd better just go home now and come back next week."

This went on all winter long, and each time the young man returned, he would interrupt the jade master less and less. In the meantime, he learned a few things. He now knew how to make green tea and how to sweep the kitchen floor with the broom. As he and the old man became friends, he began to make himself useful and help with the things that needed to be done.

As always, the old man would sit down and start talking about the green tree frog. The young man just listened now, never interrupting until the old man got tired. Then he would trudge home through five miles of snow and come back the following week.

One day he arrived for his weekly visit. It was spring now, much easier to make the five-mile walk. The jade master opened the door and told him to come in. As the student sat down, the old man pressed the green stone into his hand and gave him a cup of green tea. Again he began to tell the story of the green tree frog.

"Wait a minute," the young man said. "This isn't jade." Suddenly he knew that the green stone in his hand wasn't jade.

Priceless Gem

Maybe I shouldn't explain it. Maybe I shouldn't say that the green stone is truth. Maybe the stories I tell you have no more to do with anything than the old man's story about the green tree frog. Yet what is it that I put in your hand? The Spiritual Exercises of ECK, the word *HU*.

What you need to realize is that HU is a priceless gem, the most beautiful of prayers, a love song to God.

And how do you do it? You just sing HU every day. Just as the jade master pressed this green stone into the young man's hand, the Mahanta, the Inner Master, presses the spiritual exercise with the word *HU* to your heart every day. But you have to take it to heart, and then go about your business.

Go about your daily life. Drink the green tea, listen to people tell their stories about the green tree frog. And wherever you are, do the things that are necessary: bring in the wood, bring home the groceries, sweep the floor. Do these things, and someday you will find that you have the secret of truth in your hand, but better: you will have the secret of truth in your heart.

I tell stories like "The Jade Master" because you can take the principle home with you. It will come back to you over the weeks, I guarantee it, and probably when you least expect it. Someone at work will tell you to do this or that, and you'll find yourself trying to do it gracefully.

At the same time, if you remember to sing HU, you will realize that you have that precious gem in your hand that can show you truth and help you realize God.

This is all I have to give you, but I can't do it for you. I can only press this in your hand and upon your heart.

Co-Workers with God

I would like to thank you for coming to this ECK seminar. As you carry the principles of ECK and of truth home with you, people around you are going to be better off for it.

Many parts of the world are facing hard times now. As quickly as things ease off in one part of the world, they become harder in another; that's the nature of this schoolroom of God. Earth is a schoolroom where each of you can become aware of the purpose of this existence, which is to become a more spiritual being. It's to help you become a better Co-worker with God.

The difference between you and another person isn't that you're better, it's that you understand your purpose better. But even that is nothing unless you do something about it and live what you know. This is important.

The highest principle you can live is divine love. This is living in the spirit of God's love.

If you can do this, you will be a light to others. Often you'll be surprised when someone says to you, "Things have been a lot better since you came here." Another might say, "You came to me in a dream and explained something to me."

People will come to you and say these things at one level or another, and there isn't much you can say in return. Just realize that as you give love to God, God's love has already been given to you. Now all you need to do is accept God's love and return it to life. For in returning it to life, to your fellowman and other creatures of God, you are returning it to God.

ECK South Pacific Regional Seminar, Sydney, Australia, December 6, 1992

We have lived before. Our past lives are part of what formed us in this lifetime and put us in the circle of people with whom we find ourselves today.

7

This Gentle Flame of Love

Tonight I hope to meet some of your spiritual needs so that if you have a question about some aspect of God or the Holy Spirit, perhaps you will get an answer in your own way. Only you can decide if what you get suits you.

Each person has a different idea about God's love. Your personal understanding of divine love depends on your own experience, which is different from that of anyone else in this room. You were born into different families and raised under different circumstances, and this includes the religion you were born and raised in.

Viewpoints on God's Love

There are people from all the major religions of the world in this room tonight. As each of you were growing up, your parents passed on to you what they knew about the love of God.

It is a spiritual fact that no two people have exactly the same understanding of God, even if they are in the same religion. Therefore, no two people have the same understanding of God's love. Whereas one may speak of divine love, another lives it.

There is a world of difference between speaking about it and living it. Most of the people who live divine love speak about it very little.

The love of God doesn't necessarily come through the strongest when one is sitting in church, though I used to think it did. Growing up a Lutheran, I thought the most holy time of the week was Sunday morning, because that meant church.

Lent was also considered a holy time, but since the church service was held on Wednesday night, it was a little bit harder to feel inspired. We had to run home from school and work as fast as we could to finish our chores in time to get to church. When we finally made it into the pew, we were very tired.

Early Experiences

The minister talked as long as I do, but he was a lot louder. In fact, most of the time he shouted. During Lent it was about sin and damnation, and how we had all fallen far short. All I felt far short of was sleep.

Dad not only fell asleep during the service, he also snored. This disturbed the rest of the congregation and embarrassed Mother. He could get pretty loud. I read that the world champion snorer goes at about ninety-two decibels, which is as loud as a lawnmower. Maybe that's why our window panes rattled when Dad snored.

Besides being embarrassed, maybe Mother worried about his snoring in church because of the beautiful stained-glass windows.

Blindsided by Fear

Through my early experience as a Lutheran, I came to know that indeed I loved God and God loved me, but there was a lot of fear thrown in.

It got pretty confusing because I thought love and fear were the same thing. Sometimes the fear was so strong that I was afraid not to love God—the price was so high. I was taught that if you didn't love God enough and God didn't love you because of something you did wrong, then after you died, you had eternal damnation.

Most of the things we fear never happen to us, while the things we never considered, do happen. Life always catches us looking in the wrong direction. It blindsides us. If our religion is based on fear, we are always looking in the wrong direction anyway, so we waste a lot of precious time.

Fear keeps us from living life to the fullest. And until we can live life to the fullest, we cannot know the meaning of the awakened heart.

Home Lessons

I often learn the divine lessons through my wife, and they come by way of very little things. She once made up a list of the things she had learned from me, and it was quite long. But there is an even longer list of things I've learned from her.

Many lessons come through the gift of love. Divine love comes through human love. They really are the same, except that human love is an imperfect expression of divine love.

One thing I learned from my wife was, if you don't know something, say so.

I don't have it down perfectly yet, but I'm a man. I have to contend with training, inclination, and stubbornness. Whenever my wife doesn't know something, she asks.

Yet the cardinal sin to most men, including me, is to appear not to know something.

It's like wearing a big sign that says, "I'm stupid, kick me." No man in his right mind would wear that.

We have a water distiller at home. When the thing broke a couple of years ago, I decided to save some money by fixing it myself rather than going through the service department of the store where I bought it. So I put a lot of energy into the task. Reading the manual from cover to cover, I carefully studied the schematics drawn by engineers who understand machines but never learned the art of communicating with other human beings.

I decided it had to be either the fuse or the thermostat. I went with the thermostat because it was easier to install.

I ordered a replacement from the manufacturer in Chicago and waited a week for it to come in the mail. Then I removed the old thermostat and put in the new one. The water distiller still wouldn't work. I had ordered the wrong part and would have to wait at least another week for the right one. After all that study and investigation, I was sick of the whole thing, so I finally gave in and took the distiller to the service department.

"What's the matter with it?" the man asked.

"The red light won't work," I said. Can you imagine a man having to say that?

"We'll give it a full checkup and call you when it's ready," he said. He called a week later. I brought it home and it worked just fine.

So I learned an important lesson from my wife: Don't be too proud to say you don't know something. If you can't figure it out, take it to an expert and trust him to do it right. I listen to my wife because she is full of love. I can see how she does things in her own life that work, and that's why I know I can learn from her.

Learning Again

So three years ago I learned that it was best to take machinery to the experts. But when the distiller broke again two weeks ago, I forgot. A review of past parts orders told me that the problem was always the fuse. It never had been the thermostat. *This time,* I thought, *I'll make it easy on myself, go with the obvious, save some money.*

I called the manufacturer in Chicago and ordered a new fuse. When it arrived a week later, I struggled to get it installed properly. It wasn't easy—at least not for me. Finally it was in, and nothing happened. It didn't work.

Just a couple weeks before all this happened, I had said to my wife, "I really learned something from you when the distiller broke. If you don't know, ask." I even went into a long sermon about how hard it is for a man to admit that he doesn't know something. So I was really disgusted when it happened again this time, especially since I had reread the manual from scratch and was full of book knowledge.

When I told my wife I was going to take it to the repair shop, she said, "Let me go with you." I think she was afraid to let me go by myself.

This time there was a woman at the counter. "What's the matter with it?" she asked. I started to tell her all about the thermostats and fuse receptacles and everything else I had read. I was about to explain that it had to be the thermostat.

"The red light won't work," my wife said.

I shut up immediately.

The following week, I got a call from the electrician. "I found the problem," he said. "It wasn't the fuse or the thermostat."

"What?" I couldn't believe it.

"Strangest thing," he said. "Right where it goes into the distiller, the cord was kinked and broken."

I had to admit that I wouldn't have figured that out in a hundred years. "Good job," I said. Men like to hear that. He was very proud of himself.

My wife picked up the distiller, and the red light went on again. It worked fine.

Awakened Heart

This is also how it is when God's gifts come into our life. We get miracles, healings, happiness, and in our joy we say, "I'm the most blessed of people because God's light shines on me."

Then the first bit of adversity comes along, and faster than the blink of an eye, we forget all about God's love. We forget about our recent praises to God. We forget that God's love comes to us in many ways—through our mates, the people we meet, our pets. Sometimes just being outside on a beautiful summer day can fill our heart with the love of God.

And when love fills our heart, it becomes the awakened heart.

We suddenly see and understand all there is to know about life itself—that it is good, that it is necessary, and that we exist because God loves us. That's all there is to the mystery of life. Soul exists because

God loves It. Not because we did anything to earn God's love; we can't. Not because someone has died to save us. We each must stand on our own feet spiritually, and in fact, we do.

Disparity between Religions

There is a bond between the various religions, and that bond is love for God. The difference comes in the understanding of God. It is as different between religions as it is between the members of any one religion or even any one church.

Some people would dispute this and say, "It's not so. All the people in our church love God."

But if you look at the members of any church, you find some who constantly give of themselves to others, who are generous with their time and money. You also find some who barely leave a ripple in this world. They don't leave any of their love or pass along any of God's love, and they never have time to help or give of themselves to others. Yet, they are all members of the same church.

What causes this disparity? The difference is in how much of God's love each of us can accept. And how much we can accept depends upon our life experiences.

Why Experiences Repeat

In ECK we accept the fact of reincarnation. We don't just believe it, we know we have lived before. Our past lives are part of what formed us in this lifetime and put us in the circle of people with whom we find ourselves today.

Some people make a big thing of this and try to see into their past lives to find out if they were this or that great person. Often they do this because they feel like failures in this life. Having gone through one situation after another and muddled up the whole works, they still haven't learned the spiritual lesson that was in each experience. The next time the same experience comes along, they have to start all over.

That's what happened to me when I tried to fix the water distiller again after three years. But at some point you have to learn from your experiences.

Many people have an experience early in life which comes again a few years later with a slightly different twist. For instance, they may work for an abusive employer until, unable to take it any longer, they quit in a huff. Then they take another job with an employer who, surprise of all surprises, abuses and mistreats them. Many people have a whole string of experiences with the same bottom line.

You'd think finally they would learn from this and say, "Wait a minute. Why am I so good at finding jobs at companies that abuse me?" Or, "Why do I keep finding mates who turn out to be drunken sods? What special skill do I have?"

Those who do not take responsibility for themselves never answer that hard question. They just point the finger of blame at the last employer or the last mate and tell you in great detail why the job or the relationship did not work out. And it's always someone else's fault. But if you take a look at their excuses, you find that the reason for their failures is always pretty much the same.

You begin to see that they carefully go about selecting situations that will lead to the same experiences.

Why? Because that Soul hasn't learned something It needs to know about divine love. It could be anything. There are so many different lessons that life presents in order to teach us about the fullness of God's love.

I use words such as divine love, fullness, and so on, but there really is no way to express what it means when love enters your heart. If it has never been there before, you'll miss it without ever knowing what you're missing. But if you've ever had love through a human relationship, for example, and lost it, you'll at least know what it was like to have had it. It truly is better to have loved and lost than never to have loved at all.

Your True Identity

Several years ago, a Lutheran couple adopted two children, a boy and a girl, shortly after their birth. The man had been born, baptized, and spent his whole life as a Lutheran, and as such, he had learned that God loved him and he knew he loved God. But as a Lutheran, he never did learn who he was. He thought of himself as a man known by a certain name.

This is what I found, also, while I was growing up a Lutheran. I knew myself as Harold Klemp. If pressed with the question "Do you have a soul?" I would have said, "Oh, yes, I have a soul."

One fallacy was in the question, and the other was in the answer.

In ECK we know that the true identity of a person is Soul. You are Soul, I am Soul. And as Soul in this particular lifetime, we take on a certain physical identity with a certain name.

I used to imagine that one day I would go through the

pearly gates, and God on high would come over and call me by name: "Ah, yes, Harold Klemp. We've been waiting for you. Let's see, is that C-L-E-M-P?"

"No, it's with a K."

"K-E-M-P?"

"No, Klemp."

"Are you saying K-L-E-N-T?"

"No, not N-T, it's M-P; M as in Mary, P as in Paul. K-L-E-M-P."

This is what I run into here. If it's any indication of what you go through to get into heaven, it could be a very slow, laborious process. It could take an eternity, in fact.

This Gentle Flame of Love

Well, the Lutheran man's children grew up, and his daughter moved to Florida with her husband. About two years ago, she called him at his home in San Antonio. "We're going to go to a seminar in Houston," she said.

"Great!" he said. "Why don't you fly in to San Antonio and visit with me first? Then I'll drive you to the seminar in Houston, and you can take your return flight from there."

A few weeks later his daughter arrived in San Antonio with her husband and little girl. They all went on a riverboat ride, then out to a Mexican restaurant for dinner. It was a good day. They planned to go to bed early and leave for Houston in the morning.

After the man's son-in-law and granddaughter went to bed, his daughter came downstairs to say goodnight. "Oh, by the way, what kind of seminar are we going to tomorrow?" he asked.

"It's on ECKANKAR," she said.

"What's it about? Business or computers or something like that?"

"It's about the love of God," she answered.

"Sounds good," he said. "Fits perfect."

The man had been in a B-17 during World War II. He was very aware that the spirit of God had been with him on those bombing runs, so he knew that there was a protective force in his life.

I'll be a good daddy, he thought, *and won't say a thing.* He loved his daughter so much that he was willing to sit through the program without any opinions or disruption.

At the seminar he sat and listened for the first time as several thousand people sang HU, an old love song to God. For some reason that he didn't understand, he began to cry. He knew nothing about ECKANKAR or HU; all he knew was that he loved his daughter and that the tears were flowing. *What's going on?* he wondered. *What's happening to me?*

What happened was this: The man came to the seminar with so much love that HU had opened his heart to more.

The ECK Master Rebazar Tarzs long ago said to Paul Twitchell, the seeker, in *Stranger by the River,* "The only way to get love is by giving love." This is the whole secret of life. If you want love, you must first learn to give love.

So after the seminar, this man became the awakened heart. In time he became a member of ECKANKAR. He had never heard of it before that day, and he carried no opinions about it. But something happened to him during the singing of HU. This ancient name for

God, which is also a love song to God. This gentle flame of love.

This love also comes through to some people in the form of a healing. Unless you have the consciousness to see what is taking place, you will totally miss the love of God coming into your life.

Words

I like words. Back in grade school, we would read the *Reader's Digest* magazines that were found in the minister's garage after he moved away. We just loved the stories.

But one of our grade-school teachers had torn out any references, however vague, to sex. They did touch on the subject way back then, but I couldn't tell you about it because it wasn't in any magazines we got to read. We were allowed to read about the war, though, and those terrible ovens where people burned other people. Anything concerning sex was ripped out so the children's minds would not be soiled, but the war stuff was OK to read.

Now and then I would find a special word in a *Reader's Digest* and let it play on my mind. But then a funny thing happened: it would disappear. Even the simplest word, like *favor* or *love,* would be gone.

By the time I got to high school, I was more interested in whole sentences and what they meant. When our teacher asked a question about religion or literature, I would raise my hand and keep it up there while he asked everybody else to answer. In the meantime, I'd start to think about the meaning of the sentence I was going to say when he called on me.

I'd think about it so hard that when he finally got

around to saying, "Harold Klemp," it was too late. It had disappeared.

This is what happens to people when they talk about God's love all the time but never take the first step to loving God. And that first step is to love yourself.

The First Step

As a young Lutheran in divinity training, I would think about what Christ meant when he said to love your neighbor as yourself. I had it in my head that it meant you had to love your neighbor more than yourself because you were nothing but a dirty, rotten, low-down, lost-in-original-sin piece of scum.

The teaching said I was lost in original sin until I accepted Christ as my savior, but I never felt sure about that. The doubt kept coming back again and again.

I needed to go back to church every Sunday to get pumped up. And there was nothing wrong with that because it filled a necessary place in my life at the time. I did learn that God loved me.

I knew it in my head but I didn't yet know it through the Light and Sound of God.

Real Love in Light and Sound

A lot of people who hear ECKists speak of the Light and Sound of God think we're talking about something indefinable. They think it's as undefinable as the words grace, faith, and love are in their own religions. Not so.

The Light and Sound of God actually are Light which can be seen and Sound which can be heard.

The Light appears in many different ways, sometimes in the dream state. It comes as a blue light, in the form of a blue candle or blue globe, as a yellow light, or as a white light. White shows the pureness of God's love, blue shows the love of the Mahanta, the Inner Master. The different colors represent different aspects of God's love, and they are very real.

The Light brings more than just the experience of seeing a vision. Something happens in the heart of people who truly experience the Light of God.

It transforms them. They are no longer the same.

Karmic Circles

Their friends and neighbors see a difference, but, unfortunately, it does not always make them happy. These friends and neighbors operate in a smooth circle, which includes the little disputes and all those things that keep a group of people together, kind of like the centrifugal and centripetal forces operating at the same time. It's a circle of people in a love-hate relationship, yet this is what keeps the group together.

Why? Because it's a karmic bond. In a past life they agreed to come together, to love and torment each other to the best of their ability.

So they pound on each other, then soothe the wounds they have caused. They are simply trying to learn the Love of God and don't know it.

These karmic circles are about people being good to each other, having sympathy and compassion for each other, or hurting each other with thoughtless words, legal actions, and in any other way possible. Somebody did something to them, and they want revenge.

Getting even is the name of the karmic game, and most often it's an unconscious game. Sometimes two people meet for the first time and have an immediate dislike for each other. It's not the first time they have met, but they've forgotten.

When we come into this world at birth, we come through the veil of forgetfulness. It's necessary for the kind of experiences we are here to gain.

Soul is Eternal

Soul is eternal; It existed before the worlds existed. In ECK we say there is a beginning to Soul. God created Soul before there was time, before there was a beginning as we know it. God created Soul. Therefore, Soul exists because God loves It.

As a Lutheran child, I too understood that Soul was eternal. But because Soul and body were so closely tied together in my understanding, I thought a soul began at the birth of the individual and became eternal from that moment on. Many people believe that a soul is created with the birth of a baby.

It follows, then, that interrupting the birth process prevents the creation of a soul. This is one reason there is such strong resistance to abortion.

These people do not understand that God created Soul apart from and long before the present-day human form came about, long before the parents came about. All Souls exist alike in a pool of love and mercy. Yet, parents often feel that the birth of their child depended on their coupling, so that makes them the creator of this new life. They view themselves as little gods, giving life to a soul.

The idea that one is killing a soul is what provokes such a strong feeling against abortion. The people who feel that way do not realize that Soul, being eternal, also existed before birth.

This bit of spiritual knowledge would make this a much better world. We in ECK respect all life, but we take into account the grander scheme. We allow others the freedom to make their own choices, for we know that they, not we, must take responsibility for them.

No Strings Attached to God's Love

People often take too much responsibility for the Souls that come into this life. Taking responsibility is fine up to a point, but often this sense of responsibility is misguided. Some parents want to live their children's lives for them. They try to hold on to them even after they're grown up and married. They feel it's their right; after all, didn't they give birth to the child?

The love of God has no strings attached. Yet, the love of God demands total responsibility to God for our actions.

By this, I do not mean responsibility to another individual's understanding of God. Every person on earth has a different understanding of God. I do not want to put my life at the mercy of another person's understanding of God; nor do I expect anyone else to put their life at the mercy of my understanding.

But we certainly should have the right to self-direction, to answer directly to God—our own God.

The people of this world worship many different ideas of God. Some see God as the eye-for-an-eye militant; others think God sent someone to die for our sins. Either way, they will gladly force their beliefs on you.

So when we talk about the love of God, we have to remember that it has no strings attached. God doesn't need to have ITS will enforced by imperfect humans who haven't learned how to love.

128

These people say their God is all powerful, all seeing, all knowing. If they really believe that, then I have a couple of questions.

Why not let God handle Its (or His or Her—whatever you believe God to be) affairs in Its own way? Is your God so weak that you have to take up arms in Its defense? Why do you think God allows evil to exist?

Everybody has an answer, and for them it's the right answer. The problem comes when people try to force their answer on their neighbors, and their neighbors do the same back to them.

I say this: It doesn't matter what religion you are in; it doesn't make a bit of difference. The only thing that matters is love for God, and that means letting other people be. Give them the freedom that you want for yourself. Love your neighbor as yourself. This is the message Christ was trying to convey. If it really were understood by those who proclaim God's love, we would see an entirely different world.

May the blessings be.

*ECK Springtime Seminar, New York, New York,
Friday, April 9, 1993*

"Baby, help me remember what God is like. I'm beginning to forget."

8

If God Came Down

Often I feel so inadequate to bring the message of ECK to you, because the Light of God already shines in you. My job is simply to make you aware that there is such a thing as the Light of God and then help you become aware of your own divinity.

This would be an easy job if everyone were alike, if we were all cut out of the exact same cloth and had the same feelings and experiences. Since each of us is an entirely unique human being, trying to present a message of any sort becomes extremely difficult. This is especially so when we're presenting something like the teachings of ECK, because we're talking about truth.

By this I mean truth as I know it. Some of you will accept it as truth to some degree, and others will not accept it at all. This, of course, is the freedom that each person enjoys, or should enjoy.

Learning to Be Godlike

You cannot comprehend more than your experience in life has given you the capacity to understand. Therefore, you must recognize that while your understanding of God is sacred, so also is your neighbor's.

The title for the talk this evening is "If God Came Down," which sets up an interesting bit of speculation. There are so many different concepts of God. It's probably safer to say that everyone's concept of God is right than to try to pick out certain people or groups and say, "Their concept of God is wrong." Because who's to say? Another fallible human being?

Yet this goes on all the time. And it's the reason people have such a hard time getting along with each other. There is so much violence throughout the world, even in our own country.

My wife once asked me, "Why do people do that to each other? Why must it be?"

I said, "Simply because they're people trying to learn how to become more godlike."

She realizes, of course, that long before people become more godlike, they can be very ungodlike. Eventually they'll learn that the law of life is exacting, returning to each person exactly what that person gives to life. This we call the Law of Karma.

Attempts at Heaven on Earth

Yesterday I was at a meeting with some of the youth in ECK. I had planned just to sit down with them and listen because, like many adults, I don't always listen enough to the young people.

"Well, what's on your agenda?" I asked. "What would you like to talk about?"

"We feel that you have something to tell us," they answered. The fact is, I hadn't planned to tell them anything.

As I sat there and looked at those young people, I saw

the future, not only of ECKANKAR, but of our society; and not just the society of the United States, but of every country in this world. I said, "You need to understand that earth is really the ash can of the universe." I didn't mean that in a negative sense; I was trying to make a point.

I said, "You may do everything you can, working within the political and social structure of your own country, to improve things. But realize that no matter what you do, you will never create the great society on earth."

By great society I meant heaven. It will never happen here on earth because that is not in the divine plan.

Great Society

Back in the mid-1960s, President Johnson made a great effort to create the great society by waging a war on poverty with his Great Society program. But at the same time he set up this plan, he escalated what later turned out to be a very unpopular war in Vietnam. Both wars cost enormous sums of money. The government artfully shuffled numbers and fed false information to the public, so the taxpayers never really knew how much the government's misguided direction was costing the people. The Great Society program was supposed to create a society free from the imbalances that result in poverty.

Today you can look around and see that the experiment was not successful at all. Yet we are now embarking on another phase of socialism that I call the Great Society, part two. Why are we doing this? Because part one was a disaster.

If it had worked, we wouldn't need the social programs that are about to tax the spiritual life out of people today.

I mention this in light of the ECK teachings, which

say that our purpose here on earth is to learn to become Co-workers with God. Does this evoke a vision of people who are dependent upon a government for their food, shelter, and clothing? Can an unmotivated person be a Co-worker with God?

I'm speaking about the spiritual side of this issue as the spiritual leader of a numerically very insignificant group—and we are when you compare our numbers to those in Christianity, Islam, Buddhism, or Hinduism. We don't add up to a drop of rain in any one of those big puddles. But I'll speak my mind anyway, because it's my nature.

I want you to remember and to understand that our goal as ECKists is to become a Co-worker with God. This means that we become fully able to help in the divine plan of serving life.

Dangerous Times

Some of the ECKists, particularly those who were in Christianity before, resisted greatly when I first began to talk about the missionary program in ECK. They said, "We don't want to be involved with the missionary effort if it's anything like what we experienced before."

The practice of the Christian missionary effort, in which many of us were involved in this life or in past lives, was to inflict our beliefs upon others. We basically said, "Here are the Christian beliefs. You will accept them or suffer." Religious intolerance is a historical fact, and it was carried to the extreme during the Inquisition.

A close, objective look will show that we are again on the brink of a religious war, and this time it's worldwide. It's shaping up in the big theater as a war between Christianity and Islam.

So why do people do this to each other? They are fallible people led by fallible leaders who care nothing for the word of God.

They care only for their own power. They will do anything to get in power and even more to stay there. They rarely give a thought to the spiritual well-being of their own people; otherwise they wouldn't send them off to war to kill or be killed.

You'll find that the conflict in the former Yugoslavia is among Christians—Russian Orthodox and Roman Catholic, the Serbs and the Croats—and the Muslims. All the factions are fighting as hard and fast as they can to gain as much ground as they can. If they don't, they know that one of the others is going to do it to them.

One of the most interesting world events to occur recently was the fall of the Soviet Union. Leaders in the United States immediately jumped up and said, "The Soviet Union fell because of us."

The Soviet Union didn't fall because of the United States, it fell because of itself. The Soviet Union caved in on itself. The bottom line always comes down to money and a country's management of it. It's no different from an individual's management of his or her finances. The country spent more than it was able to produce, setting up a socialist system that took away the people's incentive to work and produce. It killed the spirit of Soul.

This is my concern with socialism and socialist programs that promise to make everyone equal. There is no equality. People do not come into this life equal, because they each bring with them a different, unbalanced book of karma. This is not to say that we don't work with compassion and try to help people in need.

But socialist programs that are legislated from the top, at the expense of the individual's freedom, are responsible for the spiritual decline of any great country.

Social Imbalance

On a radio talk show last week, the guest was an economist who was all for even higher deficit spending. He encouraged going further into debt as if it were some great thing for the country.

But a country that keeps spending also has to get more taxes from its people. The government stands in the middle and says, "I'm going to take from the workers and redistribute it, but first I'm going to keep a bunch of it for myself." Only a portion goes to the people who need it, such as those on social security and the like.

As time goes on, you find that more and more citizens become so-called needy, claiming the right to have more and more of the fruits of other people's labor.

The imbalance goes on until, finally, it becomes so great that it has to come to an end. That's what happened to the Soviet Union, the great socialist experiment, the great spiritual crusher of the century.

So what are we going to do now in our country? We are going to adopt the program of socialism, the Great Society, part two. Why? Is it good for the spiritual well-being of the people? Absolutely not.

As the government administers more programs, there's more corruption, and the people must be taxed more and more. The end result: You have less of your own money to use to determine your own fate and even to take care of your own family.

A man called in to the radio talk show and had a dispute with the economist who thought there should be more spending. Back in the fifties, the caller said, his father had gotten a bachelor's degree while working part time to provide for his family. His mother didn't have to work outside the home at all.

The economist still argued that the economy is much stronger today than it was in the fifties.

"Then why is it that a husband and wife both have to work to barely make ends meet?" the caller asked. "Families are no longer able to take care of Grandpa and Grandma like they used to. If we're doing so much better, what happened?"

The answer is that, over the years, our government has indulged in more and more spending on social programs. This diminishes the ability of those who can and want to work to take care of their own. It's impossible financially to do that anymore. My feeling is that a socialistic program takes away spiritual freedom and drives people back into slavery.

How can people who are spiritually enslaved ever become Co-workers with God? Do you see my point? Should a Co-worker with God have to hold his hand out for a welfare check? Should a Co-worker with God have to wait for Big Brother to allow this and that?

I'm not just pointing at one political party, because it has happened with both. During the seventies, President Nixon put a cap on salaries and salary increases just about the time I was to get a raise. I found out about it when my boss came up to me with a very happy face and said, "Did you hear what President Nixon just did?"

"No, what?"

"He put a freeze on wages," he said. "You won't be getting your raise." He rubbed it in a bit because it helped his bottom line for a short time.

But whenever a government, which may take the face of any political party, begins to become supposedly liberal, you will often find a heavy hand that tries to put caps on everything. At the same time, it will raise taxes, supposedly for your own good, so that you have less to spend and less ability to move on your own.

American Dream Declining

Where is the American dream where you can come here, work hard, and make something of yourself while taking care of your family?

America was developed by and for those who desired freedom, and the government can tax that away. This is a nation that in the past has stood for religious freedom, yet they can take away our ability to be an example to the rest of the world. They can take away this country's ability to be a shining light for others that says, "Give me your tired, your poor."

I feel that the socialist programs of the past two or three decades are responsible for the spiritual decline of this country, and of other countries.

If you want to measure how socialism is doing, look at the crime thermometer. The crime rate should not be rising in a country where the people are happy due to the Great Society, part one. They should be satisfied by now if the times are so much better. Instead, things are worse. Is the solution supposed to be still more government intervention to help us live our lives better and better?

More to Life

My concern is not political or social reform, because I know that earth is an ash can. It is a place where Soul has come to try out Its aggression and arrogance on Its fellow human being until the other fellow does the same thing back.

This will go on until the two finally fall in a puddle and say, "There must be something more to life than this."

Political leaders are caught up in the rapture of the fight for power because they don't understand the power of love. They don't even understand the concept; it's not their spiritual experience at this time.

The social experiment was tried on a grand scale in the Eastern bloc. There simply was no desire or incentive for people to work under a government that does, or tries to do, everything for the people.

The foreign aid that we're sending to Russia right now is not going where it was intended. If the food and other items arrive in the morning, by the afternoon it has already gone on the black market, and the dishonest bureaucrats have their cut.

This is what's happening. It's the human condition at its worst.

The Purpose of ECKANKAR

So where does ECK fit into all this? We know that it's our responsibility to do whatever we can within our circle of influence to make a better life for those around us. So as an individual in ECK, if you choose to work in one way or another at a political level, great. If you choose not to, that's great too. It doesn't matter.

The purpose of ECKANKAR is not to make political or social changes, it is to tell others about the Light and Sound of God.

The people who learn how to sing HU, an ancient name for God, can find help and comfort no matter what the political situation may bring in the future. If there's trouble in your family or at work, sing this word silently to yourself, and then let the Holy Spirit come in and help you. This is the value of HU.

We are here simply to let people know about HU and how to sing it to help themselves. HU then leads them to their own experiences, inwardly and outwardly, with the Light and Sound of God.

You may see chaos and destruction around you and know that there will never be a heaven on earth. But you can have heaven on earth within your own heart. If you can achieve peace of mind and a state of joy when all those around you are losing theirs, you have come much further than many of the people in most other religions today.

A Time of Spiritual Opportunity

I don't want to come across as a prophet of doom and gloom, because I don't see it as doom and gloom. I see this as a time of spiritual opportunity unparalleled on earth because of the present conditions. The planet is getting more crowded, people are using up and wasting resources, and everyone is bumping against each other.

They need freedom and breathing room. They don't have it, so they fight.

Perhaps what happened with the Soviet Union today is what happened to the British Empire, the Roman Empire, and any of the other great empires of the past.

But there is one important difference: They did not have the power of nuclear weapons.

Today we face a threat such as earth has never seen before, even greater than when the two superpowers— the United States and the Soviet Union stood across the line from each other, itchy fingers on triggers, ready to detonate their nuclear weapons. Several smaller states in the former Soviet Union now have nuclear weapons. There isn't even a tally of these weapons because the Soviet Union wasn't very good at keeping records. These people, Muslims and Christians, hate each other and all they need is an excuse. If too much force comes to bear on one group that happens to have access to these nuclear weapons, they might just use them.

This may not happen, of course. But if it did, it would change the world society in a way that we have never seen before.

At a Crossroads

So what do you do? Well, you do the best you can out here.

It helps to know the word *HU,* to sing it. You can also, as an individual, do whatever you can to stop the mad march of power-hungry, sometimes even insane, world leaders who care nothing for the people they supposedly represent. Having gained power, they will do everything within their power to retain power.

I usually try to talk about uplifting subjects at an ECK seminar. But I mention these issues now because I feel that civilization is standing at a crossroads today as never before.

I do think that socialism is a direct cause of spiritual decline in people in that it makes them weak. They become dependent, not on their own God-given powers as Soul, but on an outside political force that often acts without morals or ethics.

All we in ECK can do is tell people how to go inwardly and get direction from the inner source Itself, the Light and Sound of the Holy Spirit. If you never had the motivation to do it before, I would say that now is a very good time to start practicing.

Past Memories

I often feel completely inadequate as a so-called spokesman for truth, because who am I? I'm speaking from my own viewpoints and my own experience. You, as members of ECK, do not have to share these viewpoints; in fact, you may disagree 100 percent, and you have the total freedom and right to do so. But even though we may have a strong difference of opinion on some issues, it doesn't mean that we have to get into a wrestling match over them. Haven't we seen enough evidence of where that leads in the world around us?

Very angry people who disagree often get into fistfights, and sometimes it leads to shortened lives. So they come back in the next lifetime, their memory of past lives usually wiped clean. Otherwise they would come in with sticks and stones and knives, all ready for another round of fighting.

What remains is the subconscious memory of a past life in which somebody did you wrong or right. Or someone else may remember when you did them wrong or right.

This explains why you can walk into a new job and feel quite comfortable, as though you know the people. You probably have known those people before. Or it can go the other way. You may run up against someone who puts burrs under your saddle. For no reason that you can trace, you and this other person immediately start off on the wrong foot.

Families of Karma

These are the faint, subconscious memories of your past experiences with your associates of today. The human family is one big circle of karma.

Within this great big circle, which includes all the people of all the nations, there are smaller circles of karma. These include the people of the individual nations, states or provinces, cities, and neighborhoods.

There are also family circles of karma that cross state lines and even the borders of several countries. In Wisconsin, where I come from, you're always bumping into a second or third cousin. Everybody knows everybody else. It's a very strong karmic group.

So all these circles of people work down to the immediate family, the nuclear family. And within this family— husband, wife, and children—there will always be trouble. Why? Because the family consists of people learning to become more spiritual by being with others. One thing you learn is that you can't have everything your own way.

Various scenarios are played out within family circles. In one example, a boy may suffer abuse. So when he grows up, he may feel it's natural to abuse his children. In time he grows old and weak, and his grown child who has to take care of him uses that opportunity to abuse him back.

Then they all meet again in the next lifetime, ready for another round. And there is no way off the wheel of reincarnation until these people learn about the Light and Sound of God. This is what lifts them above their petty selves, above their human nature.

Human Nature

Human nature is very unreliable. People make a promise, and later, when it becomes inconvenient to keep the promise, they break it. They didn't place much value or importance on it in the first place; after all, who did they make the promise to? That person doesn't count for very much.

If you would consider that you are Soul, a child of God, you could then consider that every other person is also a child of God.

Christ spoke about this when he said to love your neighbor as yourself. You must first of all learn to love yourself. As a Lutheran, I used to feel that somehow it was wrong to love myself, because I was thinking in terms of human nature. To love yourself means to love your divine qualities—compassion, goodness, and love.

It's very easy to laugh at those who have a peculiar talent with which we are not familiar. For instance, some people claim the ability to communicate with animals by telepathy. Others claim to have the gift of healing but use unconventional approaches. When you hear of someone who calls himself a chiropractor or an acupuncturist, or claims to heal with herbs or by the laying on of hands, the first inclination is to laugh. It's easier to assume the friendly doctor from the AMA offers the only true method of healing.

But if you are a spark of God and everyone else is too, isn't it possible that someone, somewhere, has a special divine gift that you never heard of before? So, if the person isn't hurting you or anyone else, well, then, let him be. Love your neighbor as yourself.

If God Came Down

This doesn't mean you become a wimp. One of the principles in ECK is to be detached, but this was often misunderstood in the early days of ECKANKAR. Some felt it meant they should give up their families and leave. Why? Because they were giving up all for God. They didn't recognize that their first duty was to take care of their own.

If God came down, what would God do? Would God leave his family to starve while he went up to the mountaintop to pray? Or would God make provisions for his family first?

I don't have any idea what your God would do, because remember, each of you has a different understanding of God. Perhaps some people's God would abandon the family and go off to meditate. Such things, and worse, are done in the name of God.

Help Me Remember What God Is Like

During Hurricane Andrew, many people in southern Florida lost their homes, and among them were some ECKists. One such ECK family was taken in by another until they could collect money from the insurance company and set up housing elsewhere.

The hosts had a four-year-old girl and a brand-new baby. Soon after they brought the newborn home from the hospital, their little girl made a special request. She wanted to spend some time alone with the baby. At first the parents were reluctant. Fearing sibling rivalry, they wondered if she might harm the infant. But the four-year-old kept begging them to leave the nursery and let her stay with the baby.

The parents finally gave in, but not before they turned up the volume on the nursery intercom as high as it would go. Trust in God, and turn up your intercom.

They listened from the other room, prepared to run back in if the little girl gave them cause. Instead of the noises they feared, they heard their daughter speak softly to the infant. Her words were almost like a prayer.

"Baby," she said, "help me remember what God is like. I'm beginning to forget."

Many children remember what God is like until they enter the school system, even preschool, at age three, four, or five. Then they forget. They need schooling to teach them how to live in society and be responsible, of course. But at the same time, something very precious fades away—the child's understanding of God and of the people he or she knew in other lives.

Children and Past Lives

When my own daughter was that age, she said to me, "Do you remember when we were in Sweden and I was your mother?"

Children are always telling their parents what they know from past lives. But if the parents come from a religious background, Christian or any other, that does not teach the principle of reincarnation, they are not equipped to understand what the child is telling them.

"I remember very well," I said. "I also remember another time, several centuries ago, when I was a French soldier taking part in the Napoleonic blunder in Russia. I was wounded and needed help, and you were my nurse."

146

Very young children often know what they want to be when they grow up, and I don't mean a fireman or an astronaut or something else they saw on TV. They have a specific interest from a remembrance of who and what they were before. Unfortunately, these little spiritual transmitters that are your children often do their broadcasting in a spiritually dead room. The intercoms are all turned off, because the intercoms cannot take into account the fact of reincarnation.

My mother said I used to tell some wonderful stories, and by that she meant tall tales. She didn't understand what I was saying any more than most parents do when their children talk about God, about life and love. Parents assume they already know about these things and that the children know nothing.

Learn to Take Care of Yourself

I would like to make one final comment about governments that are eager to tax the workingman, especially the wealthy ones, of which I am not one. The people who favor such a law usually are those who want to live off the fruits of someone else's labor.

To them I would simply like to say, if you believe strongly in a social welfare program that can only stand by taxing the wealthy, and you believe in it with your whole mind and heart, then you owe it to your society to become wealthy. Because as a child of God, you have the divine ability to become whatever you want to, even self-sufficient human beings.

Until you can take care of yourself, you cannot take care of anyone else. This is the principle behind a Coworker with God.

These Co-workers are strong in God and able to take

care of themselves. And because they have learned how to do that, they are able to take care of others around them. These are the strong people of God, not the slavish wimps created by social programs that discourage self-help.

In closing, I would like to remind you that you are a child of God. If you have forgotten because you're older than four, you might try singing HU, the love song to God.

But remember to sing it like a four-year-old child, with your whole heart. Otherwise, you'll never find the blessings of God.

ECK Springtime Seminar, New York, New York,
Saturday, April 10, 1993

The second level of dreams is what we call the waking dream, when a spiritual influence comes into an individual's life from the other side.

9

Levels of Dreams in Daily Life

Before ECK, we often think of dreams as a super-ficial figment of real living. We wonder, *What are dreams? What do they mean?* We might say, "I had an interesting dream," in casual conversation, but in those kinds of conversations the person who's talking enjoys the dream more than the person who's listening.

You know how dreams are. We think ours are really something, and then others have to listen to them. They don't really want to, they seem bored, so we spice it up as well as we can.

Dreams and Reality

In a sense, this life is a dream. If the so-called dreams we have are figments of the imagination, well, then so is this life.

But on the other hand if this life is real, then perhaps there is more reality to the dream life than we have been able to recognize or accept in the past.

Life is real, and it expresses itself daily, whether it's in the physical or in some of the other worlds that lie just beyond the physical. In other words, those areas we go to

151

in dreams or areas that we sense by nudges or feelings which then drive us on to do something, make us behave in a certain way out here.

Influence of Images

We're surrounded by images of all kinds right here in our physical life. Negative images occur around us all the time.

The media can use images — through careful selection — to do a lot of good. Take the selection of images on the news that we see. The people who select the images for their viewers are actually directing people how to think and therefore behave. If the director or the people who prepare the program have a spiritual side, maybe they can get away with showing something that's uplifting.

But, interestingly, viewers do not generally want something uplifting. News programs like that generally fail. And so we have the news that we do.

The reason I'm speaking of images here is because it's a prelude to part of this life and also a prelude to dreams.

Propaganda

I found an interesting example of selected images. When the government of Somalia fell apart, there was all kinds of suffering and starvation. And the news media on TV every night would show us pictures of the starving children in Somalia. Pretty soon, this raised the compassion of the world and people began to put pressure upon their political leaders to do something about the starving children in Somalia. The United States and other countries got together and said, "We will ship aid to Somalia to feed the starving children."

I found this really interesting: two weeks after we shipped the food, President Bush made a trip to Somalia. And as soon as he came on TV—just about two weeks after, if my memory is correct, suddenly all the children in Somalia were fat and plump. I thought, *This is truly a miracle.*

Sometimes we look at the media and say, "Be real." They, generally, think they are the realists. But images used wrongly become propaganda. Feeding the starving is a noble cause. But when President Bush arrived and all the TV programs showed plump little babies, most of the food hadn't even gotten to the starving people yet. And I said, "They've made a marvelous recovery."

Four Levels of Dreams in Daily Life

There are four levels of dreams in daily life. Although we consider daily life not to be a dream, I'm saying that it, too, is part of the dream of God.

First there are the images or pictures, such as on the TV news that I've just mentioned. This is part of our everyday reality. The second level of dreams are what we call waking dreams. This is when a spiritual influence comes into an individual's life from the other side. An angel speaks to someone, protects someone, heals someone; there is prophecy or a visit from an ECK Master, something along this line.

A waking dream brings an influence and makes a connection for that person with some outer event. Basically there is something supernatural taking place, or as we like to say in ECK, a spiritual intervention. It will affect or influence the behavior of the individual toward good, toward spiritual growth.

The third level is sleeping dreams. Here again it's a

connection between the inner worlds which are real and this outer world. People who study dreams can become very adept at seeing how to take care of their own health, what's coming in the immediate or distant future, how to deal with relationships both at home and at work, and things of this nature.

Dreams can help you analyze your own situation and help you live a better life.

The fourth level is actually beyond the dream level, and it's the experiences that come in contemplation. Or in meditation for those of you who meditate.

Why We Study Dreams

In any of these four levels, there's always a connection between the inner, insubstantial state and the outer, physical world. And this connection has some influence on us. Sometimes it's a strong influence and other times it's not quite so strong.

In either case, experiences of the dream worlds do come through and change us. Sometimes it's for the better, sometimes for the worse. Our purpose in studying dreams in ECK is to make you a better spiritual being.

Dreams can help you in your goal of becoming a Co-worker with God.

Taking a Chance on Life

When we're young, we like to take a chance on life. There is this joy in just being alive.

I know I took chances on life years ago. I would trust the Inner Master, or the Dream Master, and I would travel here and there and everywhere—going someplace without a job simply because I trusted the goodness of life to let me survive another day and to lead me into a better life. It's a frightening thing, but when you do this you find you are truly alive in a way that you have never been before. Some experiences practically scare you to death. But when you're through them, you say, "I sure don't want to do that again. But the colors were more vivid, the sounds were more vibrant, and basically I had more love because I was aware of every little thing that was happening to me."

A young woman found the teachings of ECK back in the late seventies, and she found a great joy in telling others about the Light and Sound of God. She would give them ECK books. In her own way, while she was trying to make a living, she would travel for ECK. She just wanted to.

Going to Alaska

In 1983, after she'd been in ECK for a while, the woman was living in Seattle, and she got a nudge. Something inside her said, "Go to Alaska." Well, she didn't really know anything about Alaska. So one day she was driving with her brother, and she asked him, "Should I go to Alaska, or shouldn't I?"

Just then, he turned the car up an alley, and they passed an open garage. In the garage were two cars. The license plate on one car said GO NOW. The license plate on the other car said ALASKA.

That's an example of the waking dream. An inner nudge comes through from some source, in this case from the Mahanta, the Living ECK Master who is also the Dream Master in ECKANKAR. Sometimes people aren't very receptive in a sleeping dream, so this guidance comes through as intuition or a nudge.

The young woman went to Anchorage. When she got

there, she knew she had to make a living somehow, so she took all the money she had and invested it in a small business.

But her real purpose for going to Alaska was to be a missionary for ECK, so she decided to set up some introductory lectures on ECKANKAR at the library.

The woman was very short on money. She had put all her money into trying to start her business, and at times she didn't even have enough to buy gas for her car. One particular day she had to get to the library to finalize the plans for the talks. So she began to walk to the library, which was on the way to work.

Walking along, deep in thought, she suddenly realized she had walked right past the library.

In a sense, this woman was at a crossroads in her spiritual life. *Should I just keep walking to my business and hope to make a little bit of money so I can put some gas in my car and get around?* she wondered. *No, my first purpose in coming to Alaska was a spiritual one. It was to tell other people about the Light and Sound of ECK. So I'd better go back to the library and finish making the arrangements for the series of talks.*

And as she turned around, she saw a big sign that said Trust In God with All Your Heart. Another waking dream. This is the second level of the levels of dreams that I mentioned earlier.

Another Waking Dream

After she'd been in Anchorage for a while she moved back to Seattle for a couple of months. One day she found herself repacking the boxes which she had just unpacked after arriving home from Alaska. She started laughing.

"What am I doing this for? I just got here," she said

to the Inner Master.

At that moment another nudge came through: the young woman got the feeling that she was to go to Chicago.

"There are a couple of problems with this," the woman said to the Inner Master. "Number one, I don't really know where Chicago is. Number two, I don't have enough money to get there, and three, I don't have a job if I do get there. I'm going to need some kind of a sign to prove to me that this is really what I should do."

She stood up, walked over to the TV set, and turned it on. On the television program, a young woman was throwing everything she had into a suitcase. And the sister of this TV character said, "Where are you going?"

Of course, you know what she said. "Chicago."

It's another example of a waking dream. I'm trying to make this very clear for you so that you get an idea of the waking dream. When I first brought out the concept of the waking dream it was very difficult for people to grasp. Things would happen in their life, they got nudges, they responded to intuition, and sometimes they would have a dream where they would see the Dream Master come to them and say something, but they needed confirmation.

This confirmation would come to them in their daily life in the outer, physical world. Confirmation in the physical world of some inner direction is what we call the waking dream.

Now it becomes a matter of trust. How much do you trust this inner guidance from the Mahanta, the inner teacher?

A Matter of Trust

The young woman arrived in Chicago after three days on a bus. She had sold her car and her possessions so she'd have enough money to get there. When she got in at six o'clock in the morning, it was the start of a hot and humid day. Chicago, set on the shores of Lake Michigan, can be very uncomfortable in the summer.

But the ECKist wasn't worried. She looked in the newspapers and called a few places to find work and a room. Near the end of the day she saw an ad in the paper for a place to rent. When she called the number, the landlord said, "Yes, come by, I have a place for you."

But when she went to see it, she found a note on the door: "This place isn't for rent anymore, sorry."

It was the end of a long day, and she hadn't slept very well traveling on the bus. She was hot and tired, and there was no place to clean up. During the day she had gone to the YWCA, and she thought, *In a pinch I could stay here,* even though the rooms were all small, dismal, dark, and dirty.

At a loss as to what to do next, the woman went back to the bus station. She went into the rest room, into a stall, leaned against the wall, and cried. "I trusted you," she told the Inner Master. "I trusted you."

"Try again," he said. But she didn't know where to try again. So she went back to the YWCA.

Try Again

The young woman dragged her bags up the stairs to the reception desk, a lot more humble than she had been that morning. "I'll take one of your rooms now," she said. The man behind the desk looked at her very proudly and said, "We don't have any more rooms. This is the first time in five years we've been sold out."

She left her bags right there in front of the desk and walked off to one side of the room to have a little conversa-

158

tion with the Mahanta, her inner spiritual guide. "I trusted you," she said. "I traveled to Chicago, and here I am. But you've stranded me."

All she heard was, "Try again." So she turned around and went back to the desk.

The first man was gone and another man came out of a back room to help her. "Don't you have just one more room?" she said. "Well, yeah," he said. He was holding an envelope in his hand, and there was a key in the envelope.

"Take this to the room that's marked on the envelope," the man told her, "and if you like it you can have it."

The woman felt really sick at heart; she had seen all these dark dismal rooms earlier in the day. But when she went to this room and opened the door, she found a clean corner room with two windows. Beautiful evening light was coming in. "This is great," the woman said. "I think I'll take this one."

When she went back down to the desk, the second man was gone and the first one was back. She said, "I'll take the room." He said, "What room?" She said, "The room that goes with this key." He said, "Where'd you get the key?" She said, "From the other man who was here." He said, "What other man?"

So the desk clerk began to look for the other man. The woman began to look for the other man. He was gone. *Wow, this stuff really works,* the woman thought.

"This isn't one of our envelopes," said the desk clerk, "and what about the woman who's already in that room?" And the ECKist said, "There wasn't anybody in the room. Now can I check in please?" So the desk clerk checked her in.

The woman went upstairs to the room, and the room was so filled with love that she felt this vibration that is part of the Sound of God.

159

Appearance of God's Love

The Sound and Light of God are the appearance of God's love in your daily life in a very real way. Sometimes you'll feel a vibration, sometimes you might hear the music of a flute. These are both manifestations of the Sound of God.

People see the Light of God inwardly as a white light, a blue light, a pink light, a green light, sometimes in the form of a lightbulb, sometimes as a fire, sometimes as a lamp, or just as a globe that glows—It can be any form, any color.

The Light and Sound of God is a part of God's love that few people know about. And It's one of the mainstays of the teachings of ECK. The Light and Sound of God are the twin pillars of God's love.

This woman stayed in her room that night very happy and filled with love. She was ready to meet the new friends that she knew awaited her in this once-strange town. She knew that the love of the Master was with her.

Helping Others in Dreams

After a time, the woman moved again. She left Chicago and ended up in Los Angeles. One of her friends there was a mother who had just lost a son to a drug overdose. The mother came to work that day very distraught, so the ECKist began telling her about HU and teaching her a technique to travel in the dream state to see her son.

"How do you do it?" the mother asked. The ECKist said, "Well, you say to your master or whoever you're comfortable with, 'I want to have a dream with my son.' And then you chant HU. It's an ancient name for God. It lifts you in your state of consciousness so that you should be able to meet your son."

The mother said she would try it, but she asked if the ECKist would do the technique at the same time and be with her in the dream. And the ECKist said, "Sure, I'll try."

So the mother went home, and the ECKist went to her home. That night the ECKist woke up on the inner planes in a hospital. She walked through the corridors until she came to a room, and there she found the son recuperating from his drug overdose.

The ECKist went to him and said, "Your mother is very concerned about you."

"I'm OK now," he said. "Just tell her I'm fine." Then they talked a little bit, laughed and joked, and the ECKist said to him, "I'm going to try to find your mother and tell her that you're OK."

She left the room, met the mother, and told her that her son was fine. In the dream state the mother said, "I want to see him too." And then the ECKist woke up.

The next morning at work the mother was very happy. "I had the dream," she said. "And in the dream, I remember you telling me that my son was OK." The mother hadn't remembered the full details of the ECKist's visit with her son, or the fact that the mother had then gone to visit her son herself—just the assurance that they had shared the same dream somewhere in the other worlds, the assurance that her son was truly alive. This gave the mother great comfort.

Today is Easter, a day of spiritual rebirth. And this is, in a sense, an Easter story. Because the meaning of Easter is that Soul always lives. Soul is eternal, It has no beginning and no ending. And Soul exists because God loves It.

Dream Message

In Germany, a woman who hadn't been in the job market for eleven years decided to go back to work. Her husband was working but lately it was becoming more difficult to make ends meet.

The woman had been on her job search for a year. Every time she went on an interview, she faced rejection.

Employers told her, "No, you don't quite have the qualifications we're looking for." And every few days her husband would give her an ad that he had found in the newspaper in the employment section; he'd circle it for her and she'd call for an interview. But finally she didn't even call these places anymore because she was afraid of one more rejection.

Then she had a dream. In the dream, she and her husband were out for a drive when suddenly he pulled the car over to the curb. "My brother's over there," he said. "I want to talk to him for a minute." So he got out of the car, and while he was off talking to his brother, along came two acquaintances of this couple, a mother and a daughter.

The wife leaned her head out the car window and asked, "Where are you going?" The mother and daughter said they were on their way home. "You can ride with us as soon as my husband comes back," the ECKist said.

As soon as the two women got in the car, they began to complain. The daughter complained about a broken necklace she had. She tried to get it fixed, she tried to piece it together, but she just couldn't get it pieced together. She just complained on and on about it. The mother complained that she had been looking for a frame for a certain picture for a long time. But she just couldn't find it.

After the couple drove the mother and daughter home, they took the daughter's necklace to a friend who was a

162

jeweler and quietly had it fixed. It cost quite a lot. The husband brought it back to this young woman, but the young woman wasn't at all grateful. She just stuffed the necklace in her pocket without even a word of thanks.

Meanwhile, the ECKist's mother phoned around and finally found a frame for the older woman's picture. But the woman didn't really care for the frame, and like her daughter, she never bothered to say thank you.

The dreamer woke up and wondered, *Why did I ever become friends with those two people? They are so ungrateful.* And then it struck her.

The Inner Master said, "Look again." She realized that the dream was about herself.

The necklace meant the need for something valuable — a job to bring money in — but it was broken. She tried in her own way to get this necklace fixed (find a job), but she couldn't. The second part of the dream was the picture frame that couldn't be found. This meant that the circumstances surrounding the job were never right.

She realized that when her husband cut out these ads for her — he'd been doing it for over a year — she was never even grateful.

After this dream, the ECKist realized that the Dream Master had spoken to her to let her understand something about herself. The dream helped her understand just where she wasn't facing up to her own responsibilities. She wanted to help with family finances, but she wasn't willing to persist enough. But this dream gave her the motivation.

The Perfect Job

That Tuesday the woman called one of the ads her husband had just circled. It was an employment agency. The woman at the agency was not very encouraging. "It's a recession; it's hard to find jobs. I don't think I'll find you anything," she said. "But you can leave your name if you want."

On Thursday the employment agency called her and said, "You know, it's very interesting, but I think I have the ideal job for you. All you have to do is go to the company and take the interview." The woman who had the dream went to the interview. She got there early and sat out in the parking lot, very nervous.

"Don't worry," said the Inner Master. "Don't hang on too tightly. You've got to let go of your fears."

This is the meaning of detachment, she realized.

Detachment is something that we know about in the spiritual life. It doesn't mean not to get involved; it means to not let outer circumstances throw off your inner balance. The ECKist heard this from the Inner Master through her inner feelings. She calmed down, and she developed the feeling of a child who expects only good from life.

So when the time came, she walked into this company, had her interview, and was hired. This was quite surprising because she had been out of the job market for eleven years.

The dream helped her recognize that she had been holding herself back from a better life.

Our Key to a Happier Life

In ECK we are responsible for everything that occurs in our own life. The Dream Master will—if allowed—help you to find your next spiritual step, whether it's a better job, a mate, or what have you.

If you understand dreams and how they work, you can use your dreams to take the next step in your own life.

An effective way is to use dreams together with the Spiritual Exercises of ECK. What is a Spiritual Exercise of ECK?

A very simple one is to sing HU. Do this at bedtime for five or ten minutes before you go to sleep. It spiritualizes your state of consciousness.

And when you shut your eyes, just forget about your intent to have any kind of special dream. Just fill your heart with love, and go to sleep. Do this continuously, night after night, and soon you will find your dreams take on a different meaning.

Those of you who haven't dreamed before will find you will suddenly begin to remember your dreams. They provide a key for a happier, more spiritual life out here.

If You Smoke

Sometimes people say to me, "I'm not able to see the Dream Master, so I cannot make this connection to all the wisdom that's available in the dream worlds." And the person who's saying this is a smoker.

One of the spiritual principles is this: the Dream Master does not give the deep secrets to someone who smokes. It's a very negative habit. It's destructive not only to the smoker but to the people around him or her. It cuts off the individual's spiritual connection with the inner worlds.

So when people who are smokers say to me, "I'm just not having inner experiences with the Dream Master," I usually don't say anything. This is something they have to figure out for themselves. I'll mention it in a talk where they can pick it up themselves if they have the will or the desire to do so. But the next step requires a lot of spiritual self-discipline.

A person who smokes—or has any other habit that is detrimental to their health—feels it's an important part of survival. Sometimes a cigarette is a friend when there are no other friends. Otherwise the individual would have given up the habit long before.

I'm not here to judge. I just let people be themselves. When they're ready to give up a crutch and receive true spiritual help, they will do so. They will give up the crutches, the bad habits, whatever is detrimental to them spiritually. They'll give up these things themselves.

Dreams Can Foretell the Future

Dreams can sometimes foretell the future. In Australia a number of years ago a young boy was looking forward to seeing his first movie. An uncle and aunt had come into town, and they said they would take the two children to a comedy.

The boy was so excited. He'd never been to a movie before. But he was so excited that he got sick right before they were going to leave for the movie.

"If you're sick, you can't go," his mother said. At this, the boy threw a classic temper tantrum; he screamed and he shouted in his room until he fell on his bed in total exhaustion. Then he had a dream.

In the dream, he found himself walking in front of their house. Four houses down the street was an old Federal-style building. On one side of this old house was a door that should have led to the basement. In the dream, the boy walked to the building and opened the door, but instead of a basement, he saw a huge auditorium with blue and orange seats.

The room was filled with people, and the people seemed to know him. They waved to him and invited him to come in.

166

There was someone on the stage, but this little boy didn't understand what the man was saying. He was too young to understand. But a feeling of love came over him, and it was a good feeling. He stayed there for the entire talk, and when it was over he went back out through the door, walked back to his house, and woke up in bed.

The boy kept having this dream over and over, until one day in the physical he went out of the front door and walked over to the Federal-style building. He opened the door and saw a dirty, dark old basement.

And after that he never had the dream again. He never again dreamed of this wonderful auditorium where all the people were full of joy and this person onstage was giving a talk.

He forgot all about this until 1992. At the end of November there was an ECK seminar in Sydney, Australia. By now this man had married, had two children, and was an ECK member. He was sitting in the audience at the seminar, just enjoying everything that was going on, when suddenly this scene from his childhood opened up.

The man remembered the auditorium. It was the same one as in his childhood dream. He realized that as a child, long before he knew about ECKANKAR, he had been at an ECK seminar. In fact, he had seen the future, he had seen the 1992 ECK South Pacific Regional Seminar.

Going above the Time Track

People wonder, *How can this be? How can the future happen in this way?*

Although it seems to be a startling concept, it isn't. There really is no separate past, no separate present, and no separate future. We talk about them as such: we look at past lives that we have spent in some other time, we speak of different things we've experienced. We speak of all that as in the past. But past, present, and future are really one.

We just see things sequentially because the mind is constructed to see things in a linear fashion, along a straight line.

But people who have a particular talent in dreaming or prophecy can get off this linear Time Track. They can get above it in the Soul body. And they can see the past, the present, and the future all in the present moment because they are above time and space.

One of the preliminary steps to coming to this spiritual ability, this spiritual state of consciousness, is dream study. This is why we put so much emphasis on dreams in ECK.

Dreams can help you in your daily life. They can help you see what's coming, they can help you see why things are as they are today. You'll find you were a key player in the circumstances that brought the situations you find yourself in today.

But so often we have this narrow tunnel vision of just a single lifetime. We feel we are born into poverty as some cruel joke of God. We feel that someone else is always responsible for our state, whatever our state happens to be. St. Paul in the New Testament said, "I have learned, in whatsoever state I am, therewith to be content."

Encounter with ECK Masters

In the late 1960s a woman in Ohio was getting ready to make dinner for her family when she found she was out of bread. So she went down to the food store to buy some.

While she was there, she saw a book on a rack. It was

The Tiger's Fang by Paul Twitchell. She bought it and the loaf of bread.

When she got home, she began to read *The Tiger's Fang.* It's an account of a spiritual journey that Paul Twitchell took at one time. In the book he describes the different levels of heaven. Knowing about these levels is important because in the dream state people visit them.

St. Paul said that he knew a man who was caught up even unto the third heaven. Christianity speaks of heaven and earth as if there were only one heaven. Yet St. Paul was speaking of the third heaven, which at least suggests heavens one and two. That knowledge has been lost in Christianity; they have no idea what he was speaking of, at least from my past experience as a Lutheran.

As the woman read this book, she started having inner experiences in the dream state. At first she didn't connect them with Paul Twitchell at all.

In her dreams, she began to meet a holy man named Rebazar Tarzs. He was always dressed in a maroon robe. He would show her things that related to her daily life and things that helped her spiritually. Soon after, she found out about the ECKANKAR organization and that it was connected with Paul Twitchell.

So she thought, *OK, I'll send for some information.* But when she got it in the mail and looked at it, she said, "This is just another one of those organizations that's out to rip off people." She threw the brochures away.

When she threw the ECKANKAR information away, she was actually throwing out Paul Twitchell too; she didn't want anything to do with any of it. But she had come to trust this holy man in her dreams, and shortly after that she had another dream with Rebazar Tarzs.

Rebazar Tarzs brought a friend along, and it happened to be Paul Twitchell.

"He's OK?" she asked Rebazar, pointing to Paul.

Paul Twitchell and Rebazar Tarzs started laughing and laughing. They thought this was the most hilarious thing they'd ever heard.

Both of these ECK Masters are Vairagi Adepts, people whose only mission is to help others. The ECK Masters work not only on earth but in other worlds to help people find out about the Light and Sound of God. Their only mission, their only purpose is to help people make their own way home to God.

So the two Masters had a good laugh. When the woman woke up, she said, "I'm going to get more information about ECKANKAR and Paul Twitchell." She did, and she found there was going to be a seminar in Cincinnati in September 1971.

Wanting to Meet Paul Twitchell

The woman wanted to meet Paul Twitchell in person. So that weekend she and her husband and two children went to Cincinnati.

When they got to the hotel where the ECK seminar was to be, there was a sign that said Paul Twitchell would not be speaking at the seminar. She asked someone why not. They said, "Because he died."

Death is such an absolute term. It means that's the end of everything. That's how people think of death. But in ECK we speak of this movement from the physical body to the inner worlds as a translation. You translate a story from English to German, and the story is not lost. It is changed—and I hope improved, for those people who are translating my talks at some of the seminars for me.

The family was very upset when they heard that Paul Twitchell would not be there. They had waited all this time, and her children were in one of the first children's ECK classes in Ohio. They had all wanted to meet Paul Twitchell who was the Mahanta, the Living ECK Master at the time. The woman knew so little about ECK she didn't realize that there is always a Living ECK Master on earth.

So the family went back home. Some months later, she was beginning to get her life back together, beginning to get over this great loss of her spiritual teacher, when she had another experience.

Gaze of the Master

One morning she went to a drugstore looking for an astringent called Sea Breeze. She went up to the counter and asked where it was, and the druggist told her to look back in the corner, under the sign Remedies.

So she walked over there in that area and started looking for this astringent. Try as she might, she couldn't find it on the shelves.

Suddenly she noticed an older, smallish man standing right in front of the sign Remedies. He just stood there and looked at the sign, then all of a sudden he turned and looked at her, intently looking her up and down. *This is very odd,* she thought. But the man kept doing it: looking at her then looking at the sign that said Remedies.

Suddenly he turned toward her, looked her full in the face, and said, "Hello there." And she said, "Hi," grinning from ear to ear as if she'd known this man from her childhood and for as long as she could remember.

She just stood there grinning, looking into his eyes, and this incredible wave of love came over her. She was filled with this stream of divine love, and it lifted her in such a happy way.

171

She was standing there, just soaking up all this love, when the druggist walked up. "You haven't found the Sea Breeze yet?" he said. And he started to lead her to another section of shelves, away from the old man.

When the woman turned around to look one more time at this old man who had this power of love in his eyes, he had disappeared. *Where could he have gone?* she wondered.

She and the druggist had taken just a couple of steps away from him. The long aisle led all the way to the other end of the drugstore. This man would have had to walk down it. But he wasn't there.

As she was looking for the man, the druggist was still looking for Sea Breeze. But he was looking where he had taken her, away from this sign. He said, "I put it here right on the shelf myself last night." When they couldn't find it, he came back to the section where this stranger had been standing, in front of the Remedies sign. "Oh, it's down here," the druggist said. "I wonder how it got here?"

It wasn't until the woman left the drugstore that she began to put it all together.

When she had seen Paul Twitchell on the inner planes in the dream state he had been in the vibrant Soul body, or sometimes in the Astral body. This is a very young-looking body that we all have. But the man in the drugstore was old. Later she found out that at that time, Paul Twitchell was old. She had no idea how tall Paul Twitchell was; from her dreams, she thought he was six feet tall. But in the physical, Paul Twitchell was short, maybe five and a half feet tall.

She realized that meeting this Master, who had supposedly just died, or translated, had been set up especially for her so that she could have the Gaze of the Master.

We know this in ECK as the Darshan. This is the gaze of love, this gaze that gives the love of God to people.

*ECK Springtime Seminar, New York, New York,
Sunday, April 11, 1993*

The woman realized something: it was surrendering her opinions or her anger that allowed her to give love to her son when he needed it.

10

Love Is a Graceful Thing

The topic this evening is love is a graceful thing. I keep coming back to the subject of love, divine love, God's love for Soul.

Divine love comes to us in surprising ways, often unrecognized ways. So that when it does come, we do not recognize that the Holy Spirit has spoken to us—to help make our sojourn in this world a little better, a little more enlightening.

The Enormous Ant

Tonight, for instance, I was getting ready to leave our room, and I saw something crawling on the curtain. It was an enormous ant.

So I got a little paper cup and put the ant in it to carry it outside. And I was wondering out loud to my wife, "What is this ant doing here? What does it mean? The ECK is trying to tell me something."

There happened to be a book in the room about Native Americans and their views of what different animals, birds, and insects represent. My wife said, "Look in the book," so I did. It said that *ant* means patience. Since we'd

175

seen how big an ant it was, my wife said, "It means much patience."

It actually means more than patience; it also means trust in life. It's the patience to build slowly and carefully toward a better spiritual life.

I eventually put the ant outside, but he kept running back inside. I'd pick him up, put him outside; he'd come back in, I'd throw him out. Finally I had to throw him way out so he'd stay out. A real lesson in patience—for the ant and for me too.

Finding a Seat

At the ECK Springtime Seminar in New York City, an ECKist was sitting in the back of the hall, waiting for the evening program to begin. He noticed a woman come in, led by an usher. Although the hall was almost full, right in front of this ECKist was an empty seat.

So the usher pointed to it, and the woman—instead of going to take her place in the seat—waved toward the back, as if gesturing for someone else to come up. Soon her husband came along. The woman pointed toward the seat.

The ECK initiate who observed this said, "It was one of those loving acts between a couple." In this case the woman was saying to her spouse, "That is your seat; don't argue, take it."

I think all of you know about this, if you are in a loving relationship. The human relationship is Soul wanting to love God.

Loving Yourself as Soul

Some people wonder, *Who do you love more? And who do you love first? Do you love God? Do you love your family? Or do you love yourself?* And I say that you cannot separate divine love into parts.

Two thousand years ago Christ said, "Love thy neighbour as thyself." He was trying to get across an important message to the people of his time. Perhaps then—as now—too few people knew how to love themselves. I'm not talking about loving the little self, the egotistical side, the selfishness, the greedy side.

I'm talking about loving that part of yourself that is divine. Love that part of yourself that is divine, because that is Soul, and you are Soul.

Divine Love in Action

The man took the seat next to a woman who was there by herself. His wife was still standing in the aisle, but soon she found another usher and told him she needed another seat. And so the usher went farther down into the crowd and found a seat for her. At this point the woman who was seated next to the husband saw what was going on. "I'm by myself," she said. "If you'd like, I'll switch with your wife so you can sit together." The husband stood up and called to his wife, she turned around and came back, and the two women switched places.

As the single woman was walking to take her place farther up in the audience so the husband and wife could be together, she turned around for a moment and the husband blew her a thank-you kiss.

Again, it's divine love in action.

Life Depends on Love

There are many different elements to the path of ECK. In ECKANKAR it is my duty and privilege to teach these different aspects of the holy life.

In many of the other religions, things such as the study of dreams are belittled. I feel the study of dreams is very important for one's spiritual growth. Dreams are a doorway to other aspects of Soul in Its natural state. Soul has the ability to move back and forth from the physical world to higher planes, and It can learn to do this at will. Beginning in the dream state It can move into a higher, more alert, more aware state of consciousness, which we call Soul Travel.

Soul Travel is simply opening your heart to God's love and being able to ride on that wave. This is a more esoteric aspect of the ECK teachings.

But if someone were to say to me, "You have different aspects to your teachings, like dreams and Soul Travel and the ECK-Vidya—knowing the future—healing, and all these different things. What would you call the most important?" Without doubt and without question I would have to say, "It's love, divine love."

Everything in life depends on love. God is love, and creation exists because God loves it. Creation exists because of Souls—billions of Souls at different levels of awareness.

What Is Soul?

We are most aware of Soul in the human form, and so people in their limited state of awareness and understanding of spiritual knowledge generally say, "We have a soul, people have a soul." As I've said repeatedly, we *are* Soul and as Soul we *have* a body—an important distinction.

I mention this again and again simply because once you can understand this with your head there's a chance for it to reach your heart.

This consciousness, or this element of Soul, reaches to all levels of creation. Most people have a long way to go in their understanding of God's creation. To think—as people in the Middle Ages did—that human beings are God's highest creation is one of these self-loving behaviors of the human race. It's like saying, "I am aware at my level and I have created a God in my image, therefore this God I have created loves me more than anyone or anything else."

This, to me, is not understanding divine love. God's love extends equally to all creatures—human, animal, vegetable, mineral. If a person understands this, then that person has the beginning of wisdom.

Worthy of God's Love

I know I'm stretching the boundaries of consciousness for some of you, but I think it's an important point to make. Spiritual awareness goes far beyond the human mind. The human mind tries to put a tag on awareness and say, "This qualifies as worthy of God's love because it's called a human being. Other things do not qualify for God's love because we call them animals."

And yet as we look through history sometimes we have to ask, Are humans more like animals or are animals more like humans?

Some of the behavior of people toward people in the name of religion is filled with hatred. To be filled with anger and hatred is the furthest one can go in this life from God's love. The purpose of the ECK teachings is to open your heart to divine love.

Of course you may ask, "How are you going to make my heart open to anything, because it's open further than yours will ever be?" I won't disagree; there's no point to disagreeing. Everyone's state of awareness is where it belongs. You are where you belong; I am where I belong. Our understanding of God is the right understanding of God for us. Each person has a unique understanding of God.

But whether or not our understanding is the highest according to our evaluation and judgment, the law of life still holds us accountable for our behavior.

How do we treat God's creatures? How do we treat other people? How do we treat ourselves? How do we act? How do we think? The law of life known as the Law of Karma is the great teacher. As you sow, so shall ye reap. It's not a vindictive law; it's a law designed to open the heart to love and understanding.

Mother Knows Best

Sometimes we, as parents, have our own opinions about what's best for our children. We have opinions about how much candy the children should and should not have. We govern this sort of thing as much as we can until our children go to school. When my daughter was in the early years of school, we'd send good food with her to school— apples and oranges and all those good things. But she was getting sick, and we couldn't understand why. Until we found out she was trading these apples and oranges for candy.

A mother with three children was mentioning how the ECK taught her something about surrendering to divine love through an experience with each one of her three children.

One of her sons was twelve years old and on a baseball team. He wanted baseball shoes. But he wasn't pressing real hard for them; he just mentioned that he'd like baseball shoes. Since it wasn't in the family budget at that time, his father and mother kept it in the back of their minds.

One month there was enough money in the budget, and the mother wanted to surprise her son with the baseball shoes. So she tried to figure out what size baseball shoes her son would need.

She went to a store and bought him size five. Right after school that day there was going to be a baseball game, where her son would play. The mother drove to school to pick him up. She couldn't wait to see the happiness and excitement in his eyes when he opened this box and found baseball shoes.

You have to remember what is was like when you were twelve and got some treasure. The boy's eyes really lit up when he saw the baseball shoes. He put them on, then ran up and down the parking lot. "How do they feel?" his mother said.

"They feel fine. Just a little loose," said the boy.

Actually, they were flapping on his feet. But the baseball game was in an hour.

"We can take them back," the mother said. He said, "No, it's OK, I'll keep them." He had finally gotten his shoes, and he wasn't going to to give them back. Besides, when you're that age, you're going to grow into those shoes soon enough. But the mother said, "No, we can make it to the store, exchange them, and be back in time for the game." He said, "That'd be great."

The mother was looking out for the welfare of her children. She had been certain that her son needed a size-five shoe. The son said that the shoes flapped on his feet but that was OK. Then they agreed to exchange the shoes anyway.

So the mother and her three kids jump in the car and

on the way to the shoe store they stop at an ice-cream store. And here a second lesson began before the first one was over.

The mother would soon experience something common to anyone who has a number of kids around them: Just when you think you've heard the strangest thing from one child, another one comes up with something stranger. You keep feeling that either those children are from the twilight zone or you are.

Butterscotch and Chocolate

As they go into the ice-cream store, the mother asks, "What does everybody want? What flavor of ice cream?" She wants just ordinary chocolate ice cream, and so does one of the kids. But her daughter says she'd like a chocolate ice-cream cone with butterscotch topping.

Mother says, "The two flavors don't go. They just don't go together; they won't taste right."

Daughter says, "I want chocolate with butterscotch topping." But mother knows best. "Why don't you get a vanilla ice cream with butterscotch topping?" So the daughter says, "OK." Anything to make Mom happy. Children are smart; they know you can hold out for what you want only so long. If you keep on too long you aren't going to get any ice cream.

But when they go to pick up their ice-cream cones, a woman is standing there, holding a chocolate ice-cream cone with butterscotch topping. "I hope you'll accept chocolate with butterscotch topping," the woman explains. "Our vanilla ice-cream machine just broke down."

They drive off toward the shoe store, and the kids begin handing the chocolate ice-cream cone with butterscotch topping around. "Hey, this is really good," one of the boys says. "Mom, you want some?"

Of course Mom doesn't want some. Because Mom is right. Mom knows that chocolate and butterscotch do not go together. But the kids keep on saying, "Mom, it's really good, try some." So she's driving, realizing that if she's going to have any peace she had better try some. And it was very, very good.

The woman realized that Divine Spirit had given the daughter something she wanted—but maybe not so much because the daughter needed it but because the mother needed to learn something. The mother had to surrender her viewpoint of what was a good combination of ice cream. And because she could, then she could finally say, "I'll have a bite."

And in doing this the bond of love between herself and her children became stronger. Why? Because the mother surrendered her own point of view. The ECK, or Divine Spirit, teaches these lessons about divine love to us every day in small ways.

Everyday Examples

Divine Spirit uses small examples in your life to teach you about divine love. It does this by putting your opinion on the line—whenever you have strong feelings about something. This can especially happen with your children, because you have much more experience. And what can the children say? All they know is that this ice cream tastes good. They can see it in their mind's eye, and they want it.

And if Divine Spirit happens to make the vanilla ice-cream machine break, that's OK. Kids aren't going to get philosophical about it. They're not going to start theological debates about it. Just give them the chocolate ice-cream cone with butterscotch topping. Kids accept love simply.

If you think you are sure that someone else needs a vanilla ice-cream cone, maybe they don't. Maybe they need exactly what they're going to get: chocolate with butterscotch.

Sometimes people mistake meddling or control for love. Parents like to do this a lot; they say, "Because I love my children, I will not let them _____," and then fill in the blank. Of course, many times parents do act in the best interest of their children. This is what makes the spiritual life such an uncertain thing.

People who become set in their ways will never know divine love. They are so sure of what their small amount of experience contains that they shut out everything else in life. When I say *they* I mean *us*. We are so sure.

The teachings of ECK speak about the Light and Sound of God. The Sound is the Voice of God, and It comes through in many ways. Sometimes the Light and Sound come together to speak in the everyday occurrences that we call the waking dream. This was an example, perhaps, of a waking dream where divine truth came through in a very ordinary occurrence in life. The mother had to give up her opinions about which flavors went together.

Choosing Baseball Shoes

The family went on to the shoe store and went inside. By now, time's running out; they still have to get back to the ball game. So Mom stops at the desk and tells the clerk that they want to exchange the baseball shoes for another size. The clerk brings out a pair of shoes, size four and a half.

You know how kids try on shoes. The boy puts them

on, then runs up and down the store to try them out on the rug. He runs as fast as he can. "Yeah, they feel pretty good," he says. But he's not quite satisfied. So he sees a clerk walking around in back and asks for another opinion. "I think you could get by with a size four," says the clerk. So the boy tries on the size four. They really feel good.

His mother, possibly thinking ahead to fast-growing feet, says, "No, I think the size four and a half will fit you better." And so the son says, "OK." Just like the daughter with the ice cream.

By now it's getting close to time for the baseball game. There are boxes and shoes strewn all over the floor of the shoe store, so the mother starts scooping up shoes and pushing them into the boxes so everything's back in order. The family runs up to the desk, makes the exchange, and drives off to the baseball game where the son plays in all his glory, with all joy and happiness, his baseball shoes helping him play a better game.

That night when they get home, the mother looks at the shoes, which are now very dirty, and says, "You know, just a few hours ago they were new. Look at them now." Her twelve-year-old son looks inside one of the shoes. He says, "Mom, these aren't size four and a half, they're size four. How did we get size four?" And the mother didn't know; she's the one who had repacked the boxes in the shoe store.

That was her second lesson. She had learned again that you have to listen. You have to listen a little more carefully, and don't be so sure you're right, especially as a parent.

The same principle goes for a teacher, for someone who's in authority in government or business. When you're so sure you're right, you can almost be sure you're wrong.

I'm talking about matters of judgment, not when something is read on a scope or a meter and there is no question. For instance if the speed limit is fifty-five miles an hour, and you're going seventy-five, trust the meter.

The Brand-New Pencil Sharpener

This mother is an ECK initiate, and she's been trying to see how Divine Spirit is speaking to her every day. So It brought her a third experience with her other son.

She had just bought herself a brand-new electric pencil sharpener. When she brought it home, her son—being very much the way I was as a boy—had to inspect it. For whatever reason, whatever the law of retribution or justice is, whatever I touched during my inspection broke. And the same happened to her son.

The boy had a little red plastic peg for his battleship game. As he inspects the new pencil sharpener his mother brought home, he's thinking, *I bet this peg needs sharpening.* So when his mother's off in another room, he takes this plastic peg and pokes it in the electric sharpener. The sharpener eats up the plastic peg and promptly stops. Now the boy has a problem.

He goes up to his mother and says, "I've got some news for you. I'm very sorry, but you're not going to be happy. The pencil sharpener ate my little red plastic peg."

"Oh, great!" says the mother. "I never even got to use the sharpener."

Mom is really upset, so she sends her son up to his room. She didn't even get a chance to use this pencil sharpener, she just got it home, and now her son has jammed this plastic thing into it. And it looks as if she's going to have to throw the machine away. She's very angry.

As she was steaming about this, she took a letter out

186

to the mailbox, and Divine Spirit, or the ECK, flashed a memory to mind of something that happened when she was a child.

When she was about her son's age, her parents were away from home one day, and she decided to surprise them. So she began to dust the house. Which, of course, would have been a real surprise for most parents. On the coffee table there were these glass knickknacks, an apple and a pear. As the little girl is dusting them, somehow they bump together, and a chip falls off one.

She knew she was going to get a scolding when her parents came home. And just then her parents came home.

So she ran to a corner by the stairs and just stayed real quiet, crying and afraid. And her parents found her there. "What's the matter?" they said.

"I was trying to surprise you. I was dusting the house. And I broke one of those glass fruits on the coffee table," the little girl said, expecting the spanking and the scolding. But her parents were very understanding. They knew she had been trying to do something to help them. They could see that she was doing something out of love for them. And so they didn't scold her at all. They hugged her and made her understand that they realized how badly she felt and it wasn't her fault.

This memory came as a flash into the woman's mind as she went out to the mailbox to mail her letter. It came very quickly. She went back inside, and her son came running down the stairs, hugged her, and said, "Mom, I'm really very sorry." And with her flashback to the time when she was a little girl who had also made an innocent mistake, she said, "It's OK. I know you didn't mean it. Let's see if we can fix it."

They got a flashlight, looked inside the pencil sharpener, and saw the plastic peg jammed way back in the corner. The woman was trying to be patient and full of love. Her son said, "Let me get it out." She said, "No, get me a needle." And with the needle they were able to work it out; then the pencil sharpener worked again.

Surrendering Brings Love

The ECKist realized that if she had hung on to her anger she would have been satisfied to let that little red plastic peg stay in the sharpener. They may have tried to get it out, but they wouldn't have tried hard enough. And she would simply have thrown the sharpener away.

But because she was able to come inside with this flashback that the Holy Spirit had given her, she had love and compassion. When her son came running down the stairs to hug her, she could return his love. And they both set about trying to figure out how to undo this problem that had occurred through a child just being a child.

And the woman realized something: it was surrendering her opinions or her anger that allowed her to give love to her son when he needed it.

Love is a graceful thing. Love is always sharing, telling people who need to know about God's love in a way they can understand. In ECK the simplest way is generally to tell someone in trouble about HU. Or sometimes if you're in trouble, you can tell others about HU. HU is an ancient name for God. And when you sing it, it's a love song to God.

Health, Wealth, or Wisdom

In ECKANKAR we don't have any misgivings that we're going to have a life of bliss or that life is going to treat us better than everyone else, simply because we're in ECKANKAR.

A story I just read in *Reader's Digest* was about a dean who was conducting a faculty meeting. While the faculty was meeting and the dean was seated at the head of the table, an angel suddenly appeared. The angel said, "Because you have been such a good person I will grant you one wish. You can have wisdom, beauty, or wealth."

Without even thinking the man said, "Wisdom!" The angel said, "It is done."

Suddenly there was a flash of light and a clap of thunder, and the angel disappeared. And around the man's face and his head was this gentle glow of light. The rest of the faculty were awestruck by this visitation, and they just sat there in silence. And this silence went on for a long time. Finally one of the faculty members whispered to the man who had received this gift of wisdom from the angel. "Can you speak to us?" he asked.

And the man answered, "I should have taken the money." Sometimes wisdom is not all it seems.

Freedom and Slavery

I notice *Reader's Digest* goes through a cycle every ten years or so. It's the most amazing thing. From 1981 to 1983 and then 1991 to 1993 were recessionary times in the United States. During those years, *Reader's Digest* became more like a religious magazine with a very narrow viewpoint, pounding God at people. Then every sixth issue or so is one of their typical lighthearted ones. But most of the issues for those two or three years are put together without a sense of humor, it seems. Then as soon as the economy begins to improve, all of a sudden *Reader's Digest* lightens up.

189

I've noticed that the past few issues have been more light and happy. So I would expect with a little bit of luck from our government officials—if they don't tax the spirit out of the American dream—there will be a chance for us to realize the American dream again. A dream where government doesn't have to be Big Brother taking care of us but lets us take care of ourselves and our own.

I'm always very concerned when I see government taxing so heavily in the name of doing what's best for its people. It's making its people slaves.

This is not giving us spiritual independence. It's probably the biggest trick of spiritual enslavement to say, "We're going to tax you and use that money to do better for you than you could do for yourself." I think it's a lie. I think it's a spiritual lie, and I have very grave concerns with such thinking.

People will never realize the American dream by being on the dole. A government that takes money, keeps a bunch for its inefficient government bureaucracy, then gives certain things back to people as the government thinks best, is just like a parent who thinks he or she knows everything. Sometimes you have to let people be grownups, sometimes you have to remember the spirit of this country is freedom. And you can't have freedom when you have people's finances all tied up in taxes. I don't often speak out in this way, but to me it's a grave spiritual threat to the people of this country.

We have always been the country that the world looked to as the vanguard for freedom. Behind political freedom there is spiritual freedom, and you can tax this freedom to death. You can tax the American dream to death, and you shouldn't do it. Let people have control over their own destiny. And to do this you must let them have control over their money.

190

This country became great because it stood for freedom even though it went through centuries of many different kinds of injustice. And these injustices will continue. But the injustice of doing everything for others—that is not the way to correct the other injustices. You've got to let people help themselves. And you've got to find ways for people to carry their own weight.

Nobody else can carry us to heaven. Nobody else can help us be what we won't be ourselves.

I mention this because if anybody has a will and a desire to succeed, he or she can. I'm speaking about so many of the people who have come from nations like Vietnam, people who don't even speak English, and within a generation their children are leaders in the schoolroom and the parents have secured themselves financially. Whereas many people who are born in this country, who speak the language, are waiting for the government to give them even more and more of somebody else's sweat and effort. I say this is a spiritual lie.

Some people do not understand the Law of Life. The Law of Life is that you must earn everything that you get in the true coin.

I have grave concerns about so-called Big Brother taking care of everyone, of all society's needs. Government thinks it has the full picture of what people need. But people need spiritual freedom. People need a chance to grow. And you're not going to let people grow by taking their money from them and doling it out for things that government feels would be best for them. We've often seen this—it is a very narrow view. And it's always doomed to failure, it has always been doomed to failure, and it will always be doomed to failure. This earth is a classroom, a place to learn to grow, to become self-sufficient.

The message of ECK is this: we are here to learn divine

love so that we can become a Co-worker with God. A Co-worker means strong people, strong self-sufficient people. Not slavish people waiting for the next government check, wondering when the government is going to do more for them. Kennedy had the spirit, way back: "Ask not what your country can do for you; ask what you can do for your country." That is the correct spiritual viewpoint for this nation.

Singing HU

A gentleman had had two hernias for twenty years. And finally he was to the point where he was going to have two separate operations to correct them. But he was worried, so just before he went into the operating room a friend of his said, "Why don't you ask the doctors to sing HU as you're going under sedation?" "I don't know if I really want to do that," the man said, and he didn't.

Surprisingly, the man woke up in the middle of the operation, and the surgical team was singing some merry song as they were working on him. They had this little barrier put up over his lower half, so he couldn't see what they were doing down there.

"Can I put in a request?" the man asked.

The surgeons were startled. They don't plan on having their patients wake up in the middle of the operation, hearing them singing songs and carrying on. But they said, "Sure. What do you want us to sing?"

"How about HU?" the man said.

"Is that a mantra or something?" one of the surgeons asked. "Sort of like a mantra," the patient said, "but it's a love song to God." "Well, how's it go?" the surgeons asked. The man was having a hernia operation and he really shouldn't be putting pressure on his lower parts, so he sang, "HU-U-U-U" very softly. And the doctors sang,

"HU-U-U-U." Pretty soon it's lights out—the patient fell back to sleep. The doctors probably nudged the anesthesiologist, "You'd better pump it up." They weren't used to having their patients wake up in middle of the operation.

Remembering That Others Are Soul Too

Love is a graceful thing, and this is an appropriate title for a talk in this Year of Graceful Living.

Whenever we think we're absolutely right about something, we're probably not. And if we have a little divine goodness in us, maybe instead of being so sure and insisting upon our way, our viewpoint, we'll remember that the other person we're dealing with at this moment is also Soul, a divine spark of God.

We're very quick to remember, "Oh, yes, I am Soul." Usually this means we are the fount of wisdom, goodness, and truth—that everyone else must look to us, that when someone else begins to speak some kind of common sense it offends us. Because it's going against what we believe, it's going against our opinions, it's going against our knowledge—therefore that person must be flat-out wrong. And we are so sure about it.

If there is a crime—besides taxing too much, of course—it's growing old too fast. It's becoming so sure of ourselves.

When that happens, we've stopped listening to the Voice of God, which is the Holy Spirit. The Voice of God is speaking to us every day, in every way, in the smallest things in our everyday lives.

God's Love Comes from the Inside Out

We have much to offer people in this world. Remind yourself and others about this name of God, HU. Offer it to them. If they want to use it, fine. If they don't want to, that's OK.

There is no way that I, any other person, or any physical book of scriptures—no matter how holy—can open your heart. And whether people know it or not, believe it or not, the heart opens from the inside out. God's love comes from the inside out.

Among people who read the same scriptures of any religion, you will always find those who have love and those who don't. Some have opened their hearts to divine love from the inside, so that they could find the words of love and inspiration in the outer scriptures. People whose hearts were never opened—because they would not allow it—look into these same scriptures, and instead of finding verses that say love your neighbor as yourself, they'll find verses that say an eye for an eye and a tooth for a tooth.

It all depends upon the person. It all depends upon whether this person has opened his or her heart from the inside.

And what opens the heart? A number of holy words and prayers can, but one of the best that I've found is the word *HU*. I offer it to you and to the world today. So offer it to others in the spirit of love.

ECK Summer Festival, Minneapolis, Minnesota,
Saturday, June 12, 1993

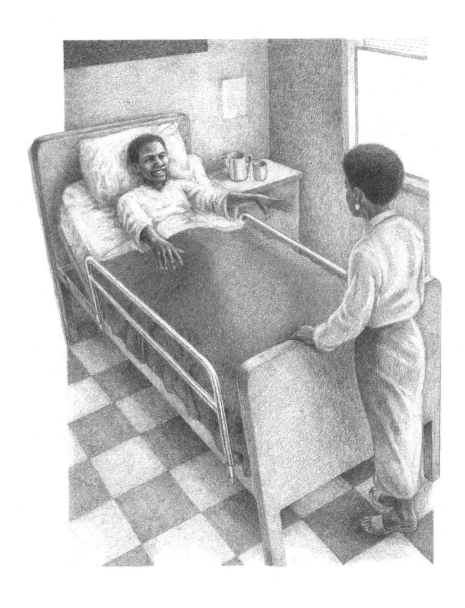

"Well, you could try chanting HU," she said. Within two days, the man's arms had healed.

11

How the Inner Master Works

Just a few minutes ago, a young man asked me an interesting question. Let's see if I can remember the tone of it.

He said that for many lifetimes, he had tried for cosmic consciousness. And he wanted to know why so many people who reached cosmic consciousness never try to go on to God-Realization. It's a good question. A very good question.

As someone said, you can always divide people into two groups: those who divide people into groups and those who do not.

Guided by Divine Love

The advantage that ECKANKAR has for you today is this: it allows those of you who truly have reached a state of spiritual consciousness to get together with others who have also done it. And you'll recognize each other.

I told this young man that people who have reached true states of spiritual awareness are guided by divine love.

There are those who know divine love. It doesn't matter

whether they're in ECKANKAR or whether they're in
any of the many other religions. It doesn't matter. They
may not belong to any religion at all. But from experiences in past lives some people understand the quality of
divine love. And these people recognize each other when
they meet. They just know, *That is a good person. That
person is charitable, compassionate.* And they can tell
these people apart from the other group of people who
know nothing at all about divine love.

The people who know nothing about divine love are
the majority, frankly. They speak of love. They have it as
part of their doctrines, and they profess to believe all
these creeds about divine love. But when you watch them
in their daily life, you can see that they are what we term
Sunday Christians or Sunday ECKists.

Going beyond Cosmic Consciousness

The ECKist who was wondering about the cosmic
consciousness and God-Realization said there were some
people in the past who had cosmic consciousness and they
felt they had reached the highest point. He wanted to
know why they didn't go further.

I explained to him how few people actually have the
cosmic consciousness state, which takes place on the fourth
plane, the Mental Plane.

I said to him, "These people who have the cosmic
consciousness reach this insight into life at some moment
in time. It's as if the curtains of life pull back and give
them a glimpse for a moment. And from this point on,
they feel they are the enlightened. They look around
and see all the other people still mired in ignorance. And
they feel that they have reached the highest state of
consciousness there is, simply because they have no one

to compare themselves to."

In ECKANKAR, people who have had the cosmic consciousness have a chance to meet each other.

Today there is this unique opportunity because of air travel. People from all different parts of the world simply fly here and there to ECK seminars; people who are not part of ECKANKAR fly to their religious meetings. People can brush shoulders with many more people than ever in the past, simply because of the advantages of air travel.

Those who have cosmic consciousness today can get together, which often they could not do in the past. For instance, a person like Socrates had cosmic consciousness. In another century someone like Walt Whitman had cosmic consciousness. And perhaps Thoreau had it too.

A person like Shakespeare was the epitome of cosmic consciousness, where the creative flow is constantly moving in a public way in the community, with plays and writings.

But if you put someone like Walt Whitman together with Shakespeare—two people from different centuries who have different levels of cosmic consciousness—they would have looked at each other and said, "Hmm." They had very different ways of approaching life. One was very reserved, introspective; the other was very outgoing.

If they had been able to meet, to break down the walls of time and walk into a study and sit down, or walk into a garden and meet each other, they could've seen how someone else with this state of consciousness lived, acted, and moved. They would have said, "Well, maybe there's something more to cosmic consciousness than the experience I had."

This would have been a reason or a motivation to look for something higher than cosmic consciousness, to look for God Consciousness.

When We Bump the Ceiling

Even today in ECKANKAR we have people who outwardly carry the higher initiations who have not had cosmic consciousness or Self-Realization.

In the material world, the physical world, it is very difficult to administer the initiations purely by inner spiritual progress. In many cases, Higher Initiates truly are Higher Initiates. But some of these initiates, after the initiation, slide backward. They become almost contemptuous of people who are in the Second, Third, and Fourth Initiations.

Needless to say, people who feel this way have slipped back since the initiation.

What do I do about it? Usually I don't do anything about it. I don't go up to them and say, "You slipped backward. I'm going to have to take that initiation away from you." There's no point to it. I allow them to hold their initiation and let life teach them better. Because life will.

People bump the ceiling. They reach a high state of spiritual consciousness and don't keep their small part of the ego or selfishness or greed in control, so they begin to bump the ceiling.

They think, "Ah, I have now reached the top." And they begin to look down on other people.

Instead of appreciating other people as lights of God, as Soul, they begin to look down on other people. They begin to think things like, *I am a Fifth, and you are only a Third. I have spoken, why aren't you groveling in the dirt?*

200

Finding Gratitude Again

We call the Higher Initiates the Brothers of the Leaf. Someone this morning mentioned that the Higher Initiates who have slipped back from their initiations, should be called dead leaves. This is not to say that people should go around saying, "Oh, you are a Fifth. Well, let's check to see whether you are a real Fifth or a dead leaf."

I don't think we should be out there pointing fingers as much as looking at ourselves. Looking at ourselves and saying, "What do I want from this life? What didn't I have before ECK? Why did I look for the teachings of ECK?"

In other words, what brought you to ECK? Try to go back and see.

What did you not find in the religious teachings you had before? What drove you from them into the arms of ECK? Sometimes you have to review the past. Try to imagine what the loneliness, the emptiness and despair, was all about. Remember. And if you can truly remember, I think you will find gratitude again inside yourself for having found the element of truth, the teachings of truth.

Talking about Truth

There are times I must speak the truth as I see it from a spiritual perspective—when I see things are going very wrong spiritually.

Up to this point the ECK membership has been used to me telling stories with hints of truth: nice, happy little stories or sometimes poignant stories of some kind or another. They relate this to truth. And as long as I never go out of character and as long as I continue in that vein, then everybody's happy.

But sometimes I feel there is a spiritual crisis facing

either the membership—as with the dead leaves among the initiates—or another crisis in either the United States or the world somewhere. If I mention this, people feel that I've suddenly gone out of character.

They say, "These are not the ECK teachings that I was used to. Harold is not teaching it right anymore."

People forget that real truth is often not pleasant. Yet the ECK has taken great pains to work with me from my childhood on, trying to make truth as pleasant as possible.

I understand a lot of you went out for ice cream last night after my talk about the ice-cream cones. Somebody was mentioning that when he looked around he saw all these people with ice-cream cones. In the same way, I try to make my talks pleasant, to get truth through in a gentle fashion whenever possible. But sometimes it's not possible. So that causes some people to feel that I've changed character. They say, "That's not truth anymore. He's now doing something else."

Finding Out for Yourself

Onstage, I'm operating and speaking as the Outer Master. But it's your relationship with the Inner Master that is all important.

There are some things out here that I can never and would never tell you, simply because it would destroy your faith in yourself. Some things the Outer Master must let the individual experience for himself or herself.

Why? Because this way the person can never come back to anyone, including the Living ECK Master, and say, "I don't agree with you because you said something about me and I feel it was not true." If what the Master is saying is true in regard to a shortcoming or a habit you have that is holding you back spiritually, then life will teach you better. And it usually does it through the university of hard knocks. This is how it works.

Ethics and Morality

Out here, I'm not often going to walk up to someone who has violated a code of ethics or anything like this. It's very difficult to create a single code of ethics for anyone.

People are all individual. Their life circumstances are unique. Some people come from Africa, others come from Australia, others from Singapore, others from the United States or South America. Within South America some come from Brazil, others from Argentina. And each country, each area has its own values.

A set of laws or ethics for one person in one part of the world wouldn't hold true somewhere else.

Out here, I am not able to say to a certain individual from another culture, "You did not act ethically." The person wouldn't know what I'm talking about. I could even take great pains to point out exactly how that behavior was unethical by high, spiritual standards. But when the person went back to his country—where such an issue wouldn't be an ethical issue—he would never have a chance to practice higher ethics.

Some think, *Higher ethics are higher ethics,* from an absolute viewpoint. I'm saying there is no absolute viewpoint about things like ethics and morality.

Always One More Step

There is no absolute way to regard the highest spiritual unfoldment, because we find those who have gone into the higher levels of consciousness realize that there is always one more step to unfoldment. This leaves us realizing that there are seldom any solid, real things to hang on to.

There are seldom any definite marks or guidelines that say, This is a sign of a spiritual being.

Some of the churches have it very clearly marked: Their holy people or their clergy wear certain gowns. If they wear a black gown or a white gown or a gown of a certain cut, you look at those people and say, "They're of the clergy. They deserve respect." I guess it's a good thing to have such an indication. Because many of the clergy today are coming under fire for moral violations. The Roman Catholic church is having a difficult time getting insurance, because it's impossible for the leadership of a church to govern the individual behavior of all its members. These sorts of problems are now coming out of the woodwork.

And we have similar considerations in ECKANKAR. Why? Because people are people. They're not all spiritually realized individuals. Sometimes they break spiritual laws, and they just plod along and hope they won't get caught. And sometimes they get caught.

Celibacy and the Church

I find it interesting that in the Roman Catholic church, celibacy was raised practically to the level of sainthood. The men and women in the Catholic clergy set forth very stringent moral codes. Today it all comes out in the open: the people who were setting up these stringent moral codes in many cases violated these codes drastically. It's not true in all cases, of course. It's interesting that the ones who were the guardians of morality are suddenly found to be the violators of this morality. Now the church has to look over this whole issue.

This is shaking the Catholic church at the very foundations of its doctrine, because celibacy has been raised almost to the level of sainthood and many believe that people who are celibate must love God more. But this is not true.

Maybe in two or three hundred years we'll have our own celibate groups growing up out of ECKANKAR too. Why? Because people are people. They're going to take examples from the past, probably from Catholicism, as Catholicism picked up the practice from non-Christian groups before it.

This sort of thing is part of human nature. Some people want to be celibate and live that way, because they can. Later other people join this group of celibates and find they can't live that way. So they violate the codes of celibacy even while they're serving as clergy. It causes all kinds of problems within the individual and then finally within the religion which was set up to uplift people spiritually.

Signs of Higher Consciousness

I spend so much time telling stories about this or that. And there's a place for stories. But there are also times to mention the expectations that the ECK Masters have of chelas, or people, in ECK.

What is spiritual consciousness? What are the signs of people who have high spiritual consciousness? Whenever you see someone acting with love, goodwill, charity, compassion, and qualities of this nature—a person who lives these qualities, doesn't just do them occasionally when circumstances seem favorable, but actually lives these qualities—you're seeing a genuine person.

Then you can say, "No matter what initiation this

person holds, this is someone living in the Light and Sound of God."

I'm pointing out the difference between those who have a spiritual consciousness and those who do not. This distinction occurs in every religious body, in every spiritual group. There are always those people who have a greater acceptance of divine love than other people—than, frankly, most people. And these people know each other.

The rest of the people are still trying to figure out, *What's my next step? When will I get my next initiation?* instead of living in the Light and Sound of God.

Light, Sound, and Love

What are the Light and Sound of God? Basically, the love of God. That's what the Light and Sound are.

They are a manifestation of divine love.

We speak about Light and Sound in words, trying to explain to people. We say, "Yes, there is such a thing as the Light of God. It's many times brighter than any of these spotlights up here. It's many times more beautiful." And these people who have never experienced or seen the Light of God will ask, "Is It brighter than the sun?" Yes, in some cases, the Light of God is many times brighter than the sun, because the sun comes from only one spot.

But the Light of God fills your entire being. It seems to come from everywhere at once. That's the difference between the Light of God and the brightest light we know, which is the sun.

You try to explain to people about the Sound of God, one of the aspects showing you that God's love is coming to you. You can hear someone playing a flute or violin so beautifully, and you say, "It's like that, only better."

206

On the inner planes, you may hear the sound of different musical instruments, birds, choirs, a person singing, all these things.

There is no way to share the true beauty of the Sound of God. All you can do is say, "Something to help you open your heart is the word *HU*." And then pass along the word *HU*.

Know the Spiritual Law

In ECK we have the connection between the Outer and the Inner Master. This talk is about how the Inner Master works.

As I mentioned, there are some things I cannot say as the Outer Master. So when people break some spiritual law, I generally don't say anything. And if they continue to hurt others by their actions—actions that come from not understanding the spiritual law—I then try to move them into another area where they can't do so much damage to other people.

People who move upward in spiritual consciousness often have more influence over other people simply because of their station in the organization of ECKANKAR. If these people are breaking some spiritual law, I try to move them into some area where they can learn more and grow more spiritually—and at the same time hurt others less.

I try to do it in a quiet way. But all the time, the Inner Master is working, trying to get this individual's attention. The Inner Master is saying, "Know the spiritual law."

Love comes from God, or SUGMAD, as we call God. It comes from God on down. And it is the express purpose of people in ECK to try to become carriers of the Light and Sound of God. In other words, to become Co-workers. Down here, we'd say "to do good rather than evil," if you want to put it in terms that are not quite accurate. In other words, to become a divine agent, to become a channel for God.

Just Listen

Sometimes being a channel for God requires simply that you be aware in a situation where someone is in pain, in sorrow, or in a state of loneliness or heartbreak.

You just listen. If you are just listening, sometimes people can speak.

And in the depths of their despair, they can find solace and comfort in someone who cares enough to listen to them and their problems. And this in turn will open their hearts. Despair and the hardships of life have an interesting way of opening the hearts of people. Sometimes just being there for people who need you can do more to open their hearts to a higher state of awareness than a twenty-minute lecture on ECKANKAR and the ECK teachings.

People wonder, *What does it mean to be a Co-worker with God? Is it to go out and give talks on ECK whenever somebody has an interest that is beyond ordinary events of this world?*

It's not always necessary. Sometimes just listen to people. And after you've listened enough, they're going to feel full. And then they're going to ask, "What do you believe?" Or, "Is there something you want to tell me?"

And then, if an opening is available, you can do whatever you need to. You can tell them about ECK and HU.

The Shake-up before an ECK Seminar

The other day storms were moving into the Minneapolis area as many of you were flying in. This happens a lot of times before an ECK seminar. There is some shake-up in the area of the ECK seminar. Many of you noticed that there were tornadoes or funnel clouds sighted in the area.

We happened to be out for a drive east of here. Suddenly the tornado sirens went off. I turned on the radio because I figured it was a good time to locate exactly where the funnel clouds were.

I figured they'd probably be right around where we were driving. And sure enough, four funnel clouds were sighted in the St. Paul area. And where were we? The St. Paul area.

Right before a seminar, every obstacle that you can imagine comes up to keep not just me from the seminar, but you too. But you drive along, keeping your eyes open, paying attention.

Put your attention on HU and the Inner Master. See what lesson there is for you from the experience. Because every experience comes for a reason, and every experience can raise you spiritually if you recognize this. Then, you will be better able to handle those occasions when things are more difficult than usual.

Exit Experience

Right after a seminar, there is often a feeling of exuberance and bliss. Not always, but in many cases. About a week later, the exit experience comes. It can be a great feeling of loneliness as you find yourself back in your daily life. You ask, "Has God forsaken me? Why do I feel this way?"

It's simply coming into balance again. When so much divine love pours into you at an ECK seminar, it's more than you're used to. And when you get home, you slowly reenter your ordinary life. As you meet people, you give out a lot of this divine love to others. Then at the end of a week, you feel empty and lonely and forsaken. You shouldn't feel that way.

Opportunity to Face Fears

Perhaps in my pointing this out, you can recognize that sometimes it's a little harder coming to an ECK seminar because the Life Force is giving you an opportunity to face your fears.

Fear is what separates Soul from God's love.

If you can work through this self-made barrier of fear that's within you, then when you come to the ECK seminar, you will find a greater degree of divine love. And this'll stay with you.

How the Inner Master Works

The following story from Africa shows how the Inner Master works. It's a good example of how one of the ECK members trusted the Mahanta, the Inner Master, to give help during an experience that happened in her life.

This young woman was going to school with a friend's family. As they were driving along, suddenly, in the middle of the road, they saw a dog. It was just sitting in the middle of the road; it wouldn't move.

This woman had an interesting description of the dog. She described it as "a dog crying bitterly." In Africa this is a bad omen. She got out of the car and went up to the dog. "Pal, what's the matter?" she said. "Why are you crying so bitterly?"

The dog ran to the edge of the road and looked back as if waiting for her to follow. So she followed. And then the dog stopped again. She came up to the dog, and he began to cry some more. The woman petted him and said again, "Why do you cry so bitterly? Everything'll be all right."

But the dog got up again and ran off into the forest alongside the road. So the woman followed the dog into the forest.

By this time, the other people were tired of waiting for her. When she looked back at the car, they were just driving away. So the woman followed the dog farther into the forest until they came to a very deep ditch. When she looked over the edge, she saw that a car had gone over the edge. Looking down, she could see there was a young man inside, and he was injured. The dog and the young man had a strong inner connection.

How do I get this person out of here? And, first of all, how do I get down the side of the ditch? the woman wondered.

So she began to chant HU, because this is a way to get in touch with the Inner Master. If you need help or protection, sing this name for God. Chant HU. So she sang HU. And for some strange reason, when she turned around, next to her she saw a ladder.

Just the thing you'd expect in an African forest. A ladder.

The woman got the ladder and climbed down into the ditch. Next she wondered how to get the car door open. She needed to tilt the car a little, and she also needed someone to get help for the injured man. So she chanted HU again.

About this time, a young man came walking past— which was highly unusual because this part of the forest was way off the beaten path. The woman said to the young man, "Can you go for help?" As the young man spoke to

her, agreeing to get help and asking if he could do anything else, she noticed, through her own inner hearing,
that the word HU was coming out of his mouth too. She
could see a light shining around his Spiritual Eye at the
center of the forehead. When she saw the light, she realized that the Inner Master had sent this person.

In a very short time, the ambulance came, and they
were able to get the injured person out of the wreck and
to a hospital.

Healing from HU

This young woman was interested in the injured man's
condition, so during the following week she went to the
hospital several times to make sure that he would be OK.
One time he was well enough to talk, and he asked her
about a number of things. Eventually she told him about
the teachings of ECK.

The man's arms had been damaged in the accident,
and the doctors felt that he would probably never be able
to straighten them again. So the man asked the ECKist,
"What can I do to help myself? What can I do for a
healing?"

"Well, you could try chanting HU because this will
open up your inner connection to the divine healing power,"
she said. "And if you are to have a healing, perhaps this
will help." Within two days, the man's arms had healed.

The parents of this young man were waiting to meet
the ECKist the next time she visited. One of the hospital
people said, "His family is here to see you." The family all
came running up to her and hugged her. They were so
grateful that she had found him in that ditch in the forest,
because his chances of being found there were very slim.
He was seriously injured and likely would not have sur-

vived—but she had listened to the dog and the dog had led her to the ditch in the forest.

A Connection with Divine Love

The woman had compassion because of her connection with divine love. She had realized that this Soul, the dog, had a problem. It was trying to get help for the young man. So the woman listened and followed the dog into the forest.

Because she had done this, she came upon the scene of the accident, and she was able to take advantage of another benefit that the ECK, or Divine Spirit, brought— the young man walking past who could go for help. And because of this, the injured person could get to the hospital where he was able to receive care and begin the healing process.

The man's family said, "We are so happy, and we're thinking of two ways to reward you. Number one, you can marry our son." The woman wasn't quite ready for that.

"Or," they said, "we can become ECKists." And she encouraged them to do that.

I would like to wish you a safe journey home and remind you that no matter where you are, as the Inner Master, I am always with you. My love goes with you on your journey home—and home to God.

ECK Summer Festival, Minneapolis, Minnesota, Sunday, June 13, 1993

In the dream, two young men began examining the accounting books. When the man woke up, he immediately started catching up on his ledger accounts. On the third day, two young auditors walked in the door.

12

Your Dreams—
A Source of Truth

I was just introduced as an expert on dreams. I'm not sure if anyone ever gets to be an expert on dreams. But if interest in dreams qualifies one, then I am an expert. I've been watching my dreams for over twenty-five years. It's been a while. Of course I started as a young child.

What Can Dreams Do for You?

I believe the study of dreams is as important today as ever in the world's history. Simply because the karma—the effects of people's actions upon each other and upon themselves in the past—is catching up.

Now it's time to pay. And this is what we refer to as karma speeding up.

What can dreams do for you? First of all, if you study your dreams you'll find that you have your own connection to Divine Spirit. You don't need someone out here to tell you what is true about your own inner worlds. You should learn how to do it for yourself.

Study of Dreams

Sigmund Freud began the analysis of dreams in modern times, but people were interpreting dreams long before that. Back in biblical days, there was Joseph the dreamer. Many dreams are recorded in the Bible. All Freud did was analyze dreams in a peculiar way.

He said that dreams are a wish wanting to be fulfilled. The censor—an aspect of your inner checks and balances—tries to stop anything in your dream world that's going to upset you from coming out into your everyday outer world. And so the censor distorts your dreams. This is how Sigmund Freud had it figured out.

Carl Jung's idea was that dreams are dreams—don't try to put too much symbolism to them, unless there's a problem. He had many experiences with dreams himself.

Alfred Adler came after Jung. His view about dreams was that you must look at the dreams in context of the dreamer. You cannot simply rely on a set of symbols and say that this symbol will apply to everyone across the board. You need to know something about the person's background. This theory is good as far as it goes too.

But in ECK we take Adler's interpretation of dreams one step further. Rather than just going into the person's background, we go way back: far beyond childhood, which is an important stage for dreams, and into past lives.

Focus on the Present

You don't necessarily say, "OK, I want to have a dream about the past." Although we do this sometimes, the teachings of ECK are more concerned with living this life today, here and now.

The past is OK, but some people get so excited about past lives, they spend all their time telling each other about how great a personage they were in history. And you know, there are at least five hundred Cleopatras loose at any time. So you take this with a grain of salt. Nobody was ever the handmaiden of Cleopatra.

All Life Is a Dream

Through my study what I have found is that all life is a dream. The dream of everyday living is no more or less a dream than what happens at night during the sleep state. A dream is a dream, but it is also reality, as real as everyday life out here.

Once you get into dreaming and move along further, you begin to realize this.

We begin dream study in ECK with the waking dream. In other words, we look at the ways Divine Spirit is trying to give us hints in everyday life to make things work out better for us.

Waking-Dream Cartoon

I have a cartoon from the Sunday newspaper. It's *Blondie* by Young and Drake. I always used to read them; I haven't lately. I believe this cartoon was printed in April, a couple of months ago.

In the cartoon, Dagwood's about to go out shopping; it's the weekend. Blondie asks him to pick up some chicken for dinner.

So he goes out the door.

First stop is the hardware store. The clerk is behind the counter, trying to ring up a sale on the cash register. Dagwood says, "Why did you say the drawer is chicken again?" And the man says, "I didn't . . . I said the drawer is stickin' again."

The next panel shows Dagwood in the barber shop. And he's seated in the chair. The barber leaves the chair, runs to the window, looks out as a woman's going by, and says, "Oh, wow! Did you see that chick that just walked by?" And in the cartoon Dagwood's looking at us with this befuddled look on his face.

After the haircut Dagwood goes out on the street, and right outside is a pay phone. Two young men are standing by the pay phone. One of them is saying to the other, "If you don't call her, you're a chicken." The other young guy says, "I'm not a chicken."

Dagwood gets in the car, and he's driving home and listening to the news. The news reporter says, "And finally eggs reached a new low, as poultry laid off." Nice play on words there.

Dagwood comes home. Blondie opens the door and says, "Honey, you forgot the chicken." He hits himself on the head, and he says, "Oh, no! I should've written myself a note."

Catching the Cues

This is a wonderful example of the waking dream, how Divine Spirit works with you and everyone else every day. Why do some people catch how this is working? And why don't others? Well, it's a matter of consciousness.

Some people are aware that Divine Spirit works in such a way. They are alert to watching for the cues that the Holy Spirit gives. This goes on all the time.

This is part of the daytime reality of dreams.

When Divine Spirit gives you little clues, little cues to

make your life better, we call it the waking dream. These come in little ways. But people feel that God and the Holy Spirit don't care about little things like this. Yet on the other hand they will pray and make demands of God, saying, "Give me this, give me that." But maybe what they're asking is not in their own best spiritual interest. Like winning the lottery.

Prophetic Dreams

I got a letter from Africa from a member of ECKANKAR. Back in 1978 he and his family had bought a piece of land, five acres in a forest on the outskirts of the city.

One day he went out to inspect the land and he noticed that people were starting to move onto the property. So he talked to his wife about this. "I feel we need to do something," he said. "We should talk to the surveyor on Monday." This was the man who had surveyed the property for them when they had purchased it. "I need to ask him about a contractor and begin building on the land immediately so that the people who are starting to trespass and take over the property know that this is someone's land. We'll build a home on it, and we'll live there."

That night before he went to bed, he said, "I turn this over to God. Give me some indication that this is what I should do."

In the middle of the night, the ECKist suddenly hears someone call out a name. He wakes up, tells the name to his wife, then goes back to sleep.

When Monday morning came, the man went to the surveyor's office. The surveyor had a guest with him in the office. The ECKist said, "Excuse me, I need a contractor to begin building on my property. I need ten men, and

I need to get going on it right now to build a home."

The surveyor said, "This man is a contractor." When he said the man's name, it was the same name the ECKist had heard in his dream.

So the home was built. Not long after, the government put up a street sign. The name of the street was the contractor's name, and to the ECKist, it was like a blessing upon a blessing. It showed him the prophetic nature of dreams and how Divine Spirit had lined this all up beforehand. It even gave him the urge to act immediately upon his plans so that the family wouldn't lose the property.

A Better Instrument

Sometimes people have a yearning to serve God. After all this is Soul's purpose in this life. If you don't know your purpose yet, it's to learn how to serve God.

This doesn't mean everyone has to become a full-time member of the clergy or anything like that. It means as Soul, as a divine light of God, your purpose in this life is to develop love and compassion and all the other divine qualities that make you a better instrument of Divine Spirit.

Where and how do you learn this?

You learn this at home, working things out with your family. Sometimes you don't see eye to eye. Sometimes the pressures of the day get to you. You have harsh words, and then you have to kiss and make up. Kissing and making up is again the sharing of love, human love, which is trying to express divine love.

And how do you learn these lessons of becoming more godlike so that one day you can become a Co-worker with God? You learn these lessons at work, you learn them at the market, you learn them through your mistakes. You learn them each time you are less than willing to listen to someone else or to be patient.

Then life teaches you better through some hard lesson. That's when people say, "Why do I have to have such hardships in my life?"

Staying Out of Harm's Way

I have a friend in Texas. About a year ago they had some heavy rains, and I knew that his dad had a home in an area where there was a dam. So I called him to see how his father and the family were.

"Are they OK?" I asked my friend. "I know they're right near the dam area."

"Don't worry," he said. "Their home is above the dam." But, he said, if he ever had a bit of advice for anybody, it would be this: don't build a home below the dam.

So often people put themselves in harm's way. Then when harm comes they ask, "Why has God forsaken me?" Simply because they—all people—are still learning how to move with the inner guidance of Divine Spirit.

Divine Spirit will help you in the direction you need for your unfoldment. But when things do go wrong, as they will, don't say, "God has forsaken me." Rather say, "God loves me so much that He's giving me the opportunity to learn this about myself, to learn how to become a more spiritual being."

Life's Movement

A young woman found the teachings of ECK about a year ago. Five months later her life went into complete upheaval. First, she had a car accident with her sister.

Then she quit one job, got another job, and moved at the same time.

But this is what she likes, she says, because whenever life stops moving she feels as though she's stopped living. Whenever this happens, she feels as if she's hit a spiritually stagnant area of living. She likes to move forward, because she feels life always has more to offer.

One night it occurred to her that above all she wanted to learn how to become a Co-worker with God. How could she do this?

She took it into contemplation, which is our way of communicating with God and Divine Spirit. We do this by singing HU or some other spiritual name or word for fifteen, twenty minutes at a time per day if we can. It's a quiet time, a quiet time with God, the divine being.

She wanted some kind of assurance that her wish to become a Co-worker with God was on the right track. She wanted to know how to go about this.

So in her contemplation, the woman awoke on the inner planes. There she met the Mahanta, the Inner Master.

Inner Master

In the teachings of ECK we have both the Outer Master and the Inner Master. They are one and the same. I don't know how to speak about this with modesty, but it's like this: if I don't tell you, who will?

I have to point out the principles here, because the principles of the inner and outer teachings of ECKANKAR will exist long after I'm gone. So although I do have to talk about these things, it is not connected with me personally in that I get a big head and say, "Wow, look, it's me." Because as soon as this would happen,

Divine Spirit would give me my lessons too.

I learned a long time ago to be a humble servant for the Holy Spirit and let it be at that. Love life, do what you can to get along peacefully with others, defend yourself when necessary, and give compassion when you can. And go on through life.

Well, on the inner planes this woman met the Mahanta, the name for the Inner Master. She was at an ECK Worship Service, and she saw thousands of people in this large auditorium. Many people were seated; they had sung HU. She wanted to ask questions about the spiritual teachings, but everybody was too busy, going here and there, doing things. So the woman thought she'd go off into the kitchen and get something to drink.

One Cup of Coffee

She goes into the kitchen and sees a cup of coffee on the counter. "I know," she says, "I'll serve the people out there. There's only one cup of coffee, but I'll begin with that." And the Mahanta was watching her, not saying anything.

She goes out of the kitchen with the cup of coffee, looks at the thousands of people in the auditorium, and says, "This is useless. How am I going to serve all those people with this one cup of coffee?" So she goes back in the kitchen. "I wanted to serve God, I wanted to give somebody a cup of coffee; but there isn't enough coffee," the woman says. "I can't just give out one cup."

I don't endorse coffee, because it has its problems. But this was her experience. Substitute tea or cola or milk, whatever you want. The principle's the same.

In the back of the kitchen, the woman noticed there was a coffeemaker going. And she found that the Mahanta

223

had filled a tray with cups of coffee. The woman asked, "What can I do?" but the Mahanta didn't say a word. He just handed her the tray.

She took the tray of coffee into the auditorium, and people took the coffee. Then she ran back into the kitchen. The coffeemaker was going full speed, and there was another tray full of cups for her to carry out.

When she awoke, she realized the meaning of this dream. It was a very spiritual dream. The meaning was that if you are willing to use the spiritual tools you have—your talents and abilities—there will always be enough coffee in the coffeepot to serve others.

Dream Help for Everyday Life

In his business a man had the responsibility of accounting for the funds of small firms. He hadn't kept his books up for a while, and one night he had a dream. In the dream, two young men came into his room and began examining the accounting books.

The dreamer was standing off to the side, watching as the accountants sat down and began to audit the books.

When the man woke up in the morning, he immediately started catching up on his ledger accounts, straightening everything out. As he worked on this for a couple of mornings, his wife asked him, "Why are you taking care of the books when normally you'd be getting ready for work?"

"I don't know," he said, "I just have this strong feeling to do it."

On the third day when he went to work, two young men walked in the door. They were auditors; they had come to audit his books. And he was ready, all because he trusted the message he got from his dream.

Tighten the Belt

I have another story from an African country where hyperinflation has taken over. We don't know hyperinflation in the U.S. When our rate of inflation goes from 3 to 3½ percent, we go really wild. With hyperinflation the prices can jump 100 percent.

Back in the late 1970s, inflation rates in the U.S. went up to 11 percent. Everything suddenly became very expensive. But in this African country hyperinflation pushed rates far beyond 11 percent. In Germany before World War II it went over 100 billion percent in just over a year. Money in a bank becomes worthless overnight. It takes a wheelbarrow full of money just to buy a loaf of bread.

Hyperinflation is taking a toll on this African country because it's a developing nation. There are a lot of political problems, and as they occur there are also a lot of economic problems.

An ECKist and his wife who lived in this country were having a very hard time making ends meet. They didn't know what to do. Some outstanding bills were about to come due, and the family needed money to pay them.

One night in the dream state the Mahanta came to the husband and in his hand the Mahanta carried a belt. Just a belt. He handed it to the dreamer.

The dreamer said, "What do you want me to do with this belt?"

The Mahanta said, "Tighten it."

So when they woke up in the morning, the man and his wife sat down and made a budget. They figured out where they were going to tighten their belts and cut expenses. And because they did this, they were able to cope with the inflation. They had taken measures to do it.

The Dream World Is Real

Freud felt that dreams are usually highly distorted because they're protecting the dreamer from unpleasant things. But in ECK we know that if you open yourself to the Holy Spirit you're going to very often get clear inner experiences. They will tell you in no uncertain terms what to do with your outer life.

The dream world is an interesting one in that it has no beginning or ending. Sometimes you'll go to a certain house, again and again and again, but each time you go back, there may be different people there.

The dream world is a real world. It's a world you live in. It's a world you live in now, and it's a world you will live in, in full consciousness, when you leave this body.

Lessons on Earth

That is why I feel it is so important for anyone who wants to overcome the fear of death to learn about the other worlds in the dream state. Because those are the worlds you're going to go to. But the distortions won't be there; you'll live there clearly. And they're usually lighter and happier worlds than here.

If you consider Earth a purgatory, then you'll probably have an equal or parallel experience in the other worlds. And you can call it purgatory if you want, but often it's a place and a time with your loved ones where you are going to continue with the lessons of how to become a Co-worker with God.

In ECK we know that there isn't just one lifetime. There are many lifetimes. If you don't learn all the lessons necessary this time, there will be other times. There is no hurry.

Soul is indestructible; It has no beginning and no end.

Path of Truth

ECK is a dynamic spiritual teaching. We have a close connection with Divine Spirit, so things happen to people who agree to this path. Or to those who have done so in the past but do not yet remember in this lifetime that they left the teachings of ECK in the past and are now simply coming back to try to pick up where they left off before. Because that's what everyone does.

Many people will come to ECK in this lifetime, stay a few months or a few years, then say, "I've had it. I don't want any more to do with the teachings of ECK." They do all kinds of things to hurt ECKANKAR.

And then they go through their lessons in this lifetime and other lifetimes. After life has taught them better, they come back very humbly—grateful for the opportunity to learn the path of truth to God, in the clearest, most direct manner that is possible.

Dream Meeting before ECK

This letter came recently. It's addressed to Mr. Klemp from someone who's not a member of ECK. This woman went to an ECKANKAR open house in one of the southern states of the U.S. Her husband wanted to go and she didn't, but she went along anyway. Here are her words:

"When I first went in, I felt like I was among people I knew. I told myself it was because they were so friendly. Then I saw your picture and I thought, *I've seen him, I know him from somewhere—must be TV or some magazine.*"

While she was at the open house, someone invited her to listen to a tape about HU, the love song to God that you sang earlier. "I realized," she writes, "that I had dreamed all of it just a couple of nights before. I'd been there in my dream. I also realized that I knew you from my dreams.

"The first time I saw you, you were on a porch and you turned to face me as I came up to you. It startled me, for I didn't know you were there until you turned. Our eyes met, and I could tell you meant me no harm. And all my fears left me.

"You said, 'I can help you.' I said, 'No, you can't. No one can.'

"You again told me, 'I can help you.'

"We stood and looked at one another, and I could read you through your eyes. And I was aware that you could read me through mine.

"You told me a third time, 'I can help you. But you must accept it, you must believe me.' You smiled at me, and I thought, *But I know you.* And you said, 'Yes, you know me. But not as who you are now. I've been waiting for you to come to me.'

"And I said, 'Where did you wait for me?'

"'Where I'm supposed to wait. You lost your way, but I knew you'd find it.'

"And I said, 'I almost know who you are. By what name are you called?' And as I tried to remember it, I woke up."

The Inner Master came to her again in another dream. She writes, "I was in a garden somewhere, and suddenly you were there and you said, 'See, I found you.' And we both began to laugh, and I woke up laughing. But I remembered your face; it was the same face in the photograph at the open house today."

"I'll probably never meet you in person. I'm writing you this just to share the experience I had with you in my dreams."

She goes on to say that she and her husband probably won't become members because her husband doesn't have the ability to visualize. A lot of times if a mate isn't ready, the other person says, "My mate's not ready, but I know about you and we can meet in the dream state."

I get these letters, but I don't often read them to you because it sounds immodest. And it probably is, highly so. I can't help it. Again, if I don't tell you about this, who's going to? I'm simply doing it to give instances of the power of Divine Spirit working through the teachings of ECK, which are alive and dynamic, such as you won't find anywhere else on Earth. This is a very direct path to God.

Singing HU to Yourself

I try to make these talks at the ECK Worship Service shorter. At the seminars, I talk longer—for fifty minutes to an hour; that's how the seminar is set up. I like to keep it shorter here for our guests at the Temple of ECK, because many of them aren't used to having somebody talk so long.

During the refreshment time downstairs, if you have any questions—whether about ECKANKAR or about dreams and things like this—ask people. Ask about what you can do to remember your dreams better.

I could recommend singing HU to yourself. Sing HU whenever you feel as if you need help or if you're hurting emotionally or physically.

Sing HU until you can get other help, because this is the ancient name for God. It gives you a direct link with the spiritual help you need at that moment.

An Ancient Blessing

I'd like to close with the blessing of the Vairagi ECK Masters. This blessing does not try to direct God's will or ask God to do this or that. It's not a benediction of that sort. It's letting things be as they are. They are as they are because that is the divine way.

We don't want to change things; we don't want to impress our will upon God. We want to understand God's will as it works in our everyday lives.

And so, may the blessings be.

*ECK Worship Service, Temple of ECK,
Chanhassen, Minnesota, Sunday, July 4, 1993*

The ECK Masters are still here. They sometimes work in the dream state, and sometimes they help more directly, if people are in trouble and need protection when something comes up very quickly.

13

The Golden Seed

The title of the talk this evening is "The Golden Seed." This refers to the seeds of the ECK teachings as they go out into the world, helping people find their own way home to God.

Looking for Peace

After the Berlin Wall came down a few years ago, the world was looking for peace. But there has been even less peace than before. People of different religions and different ethnic groups are taking every opportunity to destroy themselves and their neighbors.

There is a greater need today to tell people about ECK, the teachings of the Holy Spirit.

The teachings show people how to find love, wisdom, and spiritual freedom, and to find this within themselves, within their hearts. Because they will never find love, wisdom, and spiritual freedom in their fullness in this world.

The world is standing on the brink of destroying itself piece by piece. I say "piece by piece" because we have the capability to destroy ourselves all at once. And I guess we still can, but now the attention of people is on destroying each other piece by piece, chip by chip.

It's more important than ever to let people know that there is a way to bring peace and harmony to themselves even in the most difficult of times.

I may be wrong in this, but I feel that more difficult times are to come.

More people in the world today have their hands on nuclear weapons. And if another ethnic group is bent on destroying them, the people who are about to be destroyed will say, "Well, we have nothing to lose. We might as well use the nuclear weapons to destroy those who are trying to destroy us." It's not a pretty picture.

I hope this sort of thing doesn't come about. But people being people, many are doing everything they can to harm each other.

A few years ago the great enemy of the Free World was the Soviet Union. But the Soviet Union also provided an umbrella in its own way. The groups of people under it had centuries of hate toward each other, and the Soviet Union kept these people in check. The awesome military might of the Soviet Union could enforce peace of a kind upon the people under its domain.

Since the iron fist of the Soviet Union has crumbled to dust, these controls on the people are no more. They are free to destroy each other, group by group. They are free to take land, piece by piece.

Where we were looking for peace a few years ago, we now find there is no peace.

Why These Worlds Were Created

In ECK, we realize that this is simply following out the principle these worlds were created for.

God, through the Holy Spirit, which we call the ECK, created these worlds as a training ground for Soul. This is where Soul can work out all Its aggression, all Its hate, anger, selfishness, or lack of generosity.

So that Soul can find—in Its own way—divine love.

The Law of Karma, which is the Law of Balance, the Law of Cause and Effect, says that if you strike out in anger at someone else, then someone else will strike back in anger at you. And this goes on and on throughout the ages, as people go through many lifetimes. Finally you come to the realization that if you say you are a child of God, you cannot strike out at people in anger. You cannot use hate on anyone else without hurting yourself.

When this realization begins to come to an individual, then he's ready for the path of ECK.

Spiritual Training

It doesn't mean that the members of ECKANKAR have the last word on divine love, patience, or any of the other qualities of God. Not at all.

But if you have a certain amount of understanding that you cannot hurt someone else without hurting yourself, you have the basic qualifications to come on the path of ECK. You have the right to walk through the door of truth.

And at this point your spiritual training begins in earnest. It speeds up.

Many people who come to the path of ECK say that their life sometimes becomes harder for a year or two. But they realize the reason for that. They are paying back their debt to life. They are paying off old debts that they have created with other people, and there's usually a speedup period for a short time.

After people get used to the way of ECK, after a few months or a year or so, things come back into harmony. And life goes on as before.

Qualifying for an Initiation

After a year or two in ECK, a person qualifies for an ECK initiation.

In the first year of study an individual is ready for the First Initiation. This is the dream initiation.

It happens completely in the dream state, in your dreams. The Inner Master comes to you and gives you some sort of experience to make you a more pure channel, a more pure spiritual being.

There are many spiritual beings who have the duty of helping people find the path of ECK. We call these people the ECK Masters. They are the ones who help the spiritual leader of ECKANKAR find those who are ready to walk the true path to God.

True Path

When I say "true path," I don't mean true in the sense that other paths are not true. Each path is true in its own way. Christianity has its own lessons to teach. Islam has lessons to teach its people. And one of the main lessons within each group is the fundamentals of divine love.

But even though this is a principle of a religion, it does not mean that most of the members are practicing that principle.

It is simply the spiritual ideal that these people are looking toward.

If people take the trouble to belong to a religion, it may be for social reasons or because they were born into that religion. But they are a part of it, and it shapes them. The religion shapes their feelings and their thoughts.

I wish it were always the case that a religion shaped people into more spiritual beings. A religion will do that until it tries to force its ways upon those who do not want the religion. This, to me, is a violation of spiritual law.

Missionaries

We have missionaries in ECK who go out and present the ECK teachings to others, saying, "Here are the teachings of the Light and Sound of God. They are here to help you find your own way home." Some religions have missionaries who say, "This is the right way, and if you do not follow it you shall be damned."

This puts fear into people, and it's not at all true. It is a violation of spiritual law to put fear into the hearts of people to make them a member of your faith.

It's bad enough that this sort of fear is communicated through words. Sometimes the missionaries feel they must go a step farther. They torture people, force people, imprison people if they will not come into the religion of the missionaries. This is the most severe violation of spiritual law that one can imagine.

It shows which people in that religion are not spiritual at all, which people do not know the divine law of God.

Teachings of Divine Love

I am here with the teachings of ECK to point out the teachings of divine love.

Divine love begins first with yourself. Until you learn to love yourself, you cannot love someone else. Until you learn to love yourself, you cannot even love God.

So it begins with you.

But I'm speaking about divine love; I'm not speaking about vanity, or any of the other kinds of selfish love that are part of human nature—the negative traits that people have as they come here to earth to learn how to become more perfect channels, or vehicles, or Co-workers with God.

Those who help find the seeker are known as the ECK Masters. In the ECK teachings we have a number of ECK Masters who help me reach you. This is our missionary program.

I try to bring the ECK teachings to people in the world. There are ECK initiates who help with this task. The ECK Masters usually work in the dream state or meet people who are new to ECK. They come to you when you are ready, to help you take another step in your own spiritual search.

Seeing Rebazar Tarzs

I got a letter from an individual in Australia. He has been writing to me for the past few months.

He'd been looking for a teaching position, and finally he got a very good position in Kuwait. He'll be making the journey soon, hoping to start teaching this fall. But while he was waiting for some word about what his future would be, he spent time at the ECK center and had some wonderful conversations with people who came there to talk about the ECK principles.

One day a man came up the steps to the ECK center, shouting at the top of his voice, "I can't believe it! I can't believe it!"

As the man came up the stairs, this teacher who was

tending the ECK center asked him, "What can't you believe?"

"Two days ago I had a dream," the man said, "and this man with a beard came and with him there was this shining blue light." Remember, we are the teaching of the Sound and Light.

He said, "This man was very striking. His picture is one of these portraits that you have hanging on the wall."

The teacher who was tending the ECK center said, "Which one of them did you see in your dream?" The man pointed to the picture of Rebazar Tarzs, a Tibetan ECK Master who served as spiritual leader for the ECK teachings several centuries ago.

Help from ECK Masters

These ECK Masters are still here. They sometimes work in the dream state, and sometimes they help more directly, if people are in trouble and need protection when something comes up very quickly.

These Masters are here to help you.

When the time is right and you need the help, you will find someone like Rebazar Tarzs or Paul Twitchell, who founded the modern-day teachings of ECKANKAR. They will come, and they'll help you.

You may wonder, *Why would these people help me, a stranger?* Sometimes people ask me about this, saying, "After all, I'm a Christian. I don't believe in ECK Masters." But remember that one of the principles in ECK is reincarnation. Nearly 99 percent of the people who come to ECK in this lifetime have been a follower of ECK in the past under one of these ECK Masters.

We provide pictures of the ECK Masters for this reason. Some of them are in our books; sometimes we have them available in other ways, like at the ECK centers. We do this for the new people, those who come to ECKANKAR for the first time, so that they may recognize one of their dream teachers.

These dream teachers, the ECK Masters, are often with people for their entire lives—long before they've ever heard of ECKANKAR.

Inner Connection

When people are interested in becoming a member of ECK, we let them know the requested donation for membership. In Minneapolis, we have a staff that takes care of all the paperwork. One day a staff member made a mistake while handling the donation of one of the members of ECKANKAR.

The staff member knew that when the paperwork got to the ECKist there would be a misunderstanding. There would possibly be some hard feelings. So this woman on the ECK staff tried to stop the letter.

But it had already gone out in the mail. Three days had passed before she had caught the error.

The staff member decided to call the ECKist at her home in Canada. She identified herself then said, "I made a mistake with your membership. I've straightened it out, so please don't worry; everything is in order."

The woman in Canada had just that morning received the letter with her ECK discourses for the month. She read about the mix-up in her membership.

Even members of ECK become upset, this being very natural and very human.

She was very upset about it, but when she went into contemplation, Paul Twitchell, who translated, or died, back in 1971, came to her on the inner. "Don't worry about it," he said. "It was a mistake; they're going to fix the error, so take it easy and don't get upset."

Just after this had happened, the phone rang. It was the person from the ECKANKAR Spiritual Center apologizing for the error.

A Different Kind of Path to Truth

In the teachings of ECKANKAR, the Religion of the Light and Sound of God, you're going to be exposed to a different kind of path to truth than you have ever experienced before.

There will be this inner-outer connection.

I'm not saying that people are going to be helping you out every day, minute by minute. That's not what this path is about. If the Masters did everything for you and made all your decisions for you, how could you grow spiritually?

But sometimes it happens, in exceptional cases—and for some people this may only happen once in twenty years, while other people may have experiences like this every week. It depends upon the individual. It depends upon you.

It depends upon how much help you need just then, how much strength you need, how much divine love you need.

It all depends upon you, because ultimately this teaching of ECK is an individual path.

Tailoring the Teachings

Out here we have books and discourses, monthly letters from me to you. I also write to many people in personal letters.

241

I try to speak to your heart and to your spiritual needs. I try to be a spiritual teacher.

I feel I fail so often. I'll write a discourse and try to give some principle of truth to you as clearly as possible. Then some people will criticize me and say, "This is too simple." And other people will say, "This is too complicated." On the outside, I am trying to give a teaching to so many different levels of consciousness.

But on the inside, as the inner teacher, I can custom fit the teachings to you, to give you the experiences that you need in your dreams.

Sometimes I give you the experiences that you need in your outer life, when you're miles away from the Living ECK Master. When something happens there'll be a connection at work, at home with friends, and you're going to know that the hand of God was in this. The hand of the Divine was here.

Becoming One with the Holy Spirit

I do not claim I am God, or something like this. It's impossible for any human being to become God. It's almost ridiculous to think of it, but some of the Eastern paths say, "Study with us, and you shall become one with God."

Our position is different. Our aim is to become one with the Holy Spirit. Because the Holy Spirit is the Light and Sound of God.

We can become one with the Light and Sound, we can become one with the Holy Spirit, but not one with God.

God, or SUGMAD, is the creator. But creation came about through the Voice of God, or the Word, which is the Holy Spirit. And we can become one with the Holy Spirit.

I want to make this distinction clear for you.

Seeing the Past

Sometimes people wonder why they were born into a certain family. And if you're raised in a Christian, Jewish, or Islamic family, the answer isn't always clear.

A member of ECK in New York City has been afraid of icebergs since she was a child. To go from one area of the city to another she often had to ride the ferry, and she did not like the boat ride. Nor did she like to swim over rocks. One vacation in Puerto Rico, the tide caught her and swept her out over some rocks; she panicked and nearly drowned.

The woman always wondered why she had this fear of rocks in the water, and this dislike of boats.

This fear grew stronger as she grew into adulthood. By the time she became an adult she absolutely could not stand to look at pictures of icebergs at all.

At one of her ECK classes, they did a spiritual exercise to look into the past—for those who wanted to do it for themselves. As they did the exercise, the woman wondered, *Is it possible that I was on the* Titanic *when it sank at the turn of the century?* So she went into contemplation, and she began to see the past. But before she could see the outcome, she cut off the experience and just sat in the room waiting for everybody else to finish with their spiritual exercise.

The next night at bedtime, she was doing her daily contemplation. The Inner Master came to her and said, "Why did you cut off the contemplation yesterday?"

"I just felt uncomfortable, and I didn't want to see any more," the woman said.

"It's important for you to see and know what's happened in the past," the Master said, "so that you can live this life without fear."

243

Our Karma at Birth

When fear is a dominant force in your life, it takes away the joy and freedom of living.

There are all these hidden fears—stacks and stacks, piles and piles of these fears—inside each human being. And where do they come from? Many of them come from before your birth into this lifetime.

Each human being has had hundreds and even thousands of past lives. Plenty of time to find an opportunity to hurt others and to have others hurt you back. You get hurt often enough in a certain way, and you become afraid of that sort of pain.

People are not equal when they come to this world at birth. Everyone has a different load of karma coming into this lifetime.

But most people have no idea how to work this off, or that it even exists. And so they live within their human shells, too afraid to live yet too afraid to die. Wanting heaven, because earth is hell, and afraid to go to heaven, because you have to die to get there.

It's this big spiritual problem.

Titanic Memory

This woman went into contemplation again. The Inner Master let her see the past like a movie, as if she had become an actress in this movie. She saw that she was indeed on the *Titanic*.

But she didn't die on the *Titanic*. She was one of the women who was able to get into a lifeboat and was thus able to save her life. There were men in the water who wanted to climb into the lifeboat, and she wouldn't let them come in. She feared it would have sunk the lifeboat and threatened her own life.

In this present lifetime the woman gave birth to two healthy children, but after these full-term pregnancies she had four boys in a row who died near birth. Each lived just a few hours to a few days before they died, and she couldn't understand this.

In her contemplation, she saw that when she wouldn't let the men in the water get into the lifeboats, she was being very selfish and denying others the right to life. And so in her present life, she lost four children in a row, shortly after birth. She also realized that she had been born into a family that did not prize generosity, a very selfish family.

What Family Will You Join?

People wonder how they get into the families they get into.

It's always the Lords of Karma who make the final decision between lifetimes. Or, if you are ready for the path of ECK, the Inner Master and the Lords of Karma decide together which setting, which group of people from your past would be best for you to join as a family, so that you can have the best spiritual opportunity in this lifetime.

The best spiritual opportunity is not necessarily the easiest life.

I think many of you will agree that your life has been anything but easy. In fact for many it has been very hard. Sometimes the best way to learn the spiritual lessons is through a life of hardship.

I had my hardships when I was growing up. I have my hardships today. Life will either crush you, or you will rise above life, to live more fully and with more joy.

245

Sometimes it's difficult. Many people are in different stages of health, different ages of life.

We don't try to shortchange aging, because we know it's part of the process. We do what we can to be strong, to retain our health as long as possible. We use our God-given creativity and our ability to listen and to learn to extend our life as long as possible. We do whatever we can to make this a rich life, to make it worth the trouble.

Eternity in a Day

I remember at one, two, or three years old, each day seemed to take an eternity. For instance, if my mother said, "Take a nap," she could only make us lie down for two or three hours, but it seemed to us like two days.

I would just lie there and think, *There goes my life.*

Parents don't know that, because time is entirely different for a child than it is for an adult.

On the plane coming to the seminar, there was a young woman, still in her late teens, with a very young child. Neither of them were used to sitting on a plane for six or seven hours. The mother was so young that it was a real test of endurance for her.

She had more problems with her temper than her child of four did.

Although the mother was upset, the child was just beautiful and, for the most part, good throughout the long flight. For the child it was probably a flight of three days. For the mother it was probably a flight of three days too.

Journey to Africa

Next week is the ECK African Seminar. Peter Skelskey, president of ECKANKAR, is going to be there. Some people think, "It must be really nice to be working in the leadership of ECKANKAR; they have it made." They don't know the real story.

I won't go into his hardships right now, because he usually keeps them to himself. Me, I blab all over the place, but other people keep it to themselves.

Peter's had a number of hardships, and in a way it's almost fitting if you're going to speak in Africa that you have hardships on your way over. Otherwise you will not understand the situation of the people there.

We have hard times here. But in a developing country, what the ECK members go through is beyond belief.

I will also say this: their connection with the Inner Master is sometimes ten times stronger in Africa than it is in any other part of the world—including the United States, Europe, or Canada.

They don't have the protection of a stable society; sometimes brute force is the rule. In Africa, the people are having to establish and develop a country and go through all the painful steps that many of us in the States did two hundred years ago. Here in Europe, your countries go back even further into the past, through many centuries.

You go through these cycles.

In this lifetime someone happens to come from Germany, England, France, Nigeria, or Holland. It doesn't matter. As Soul, you've been in practically every country of the world before you come to the path of ECK. You've lived enough lifetimes to have done this.

Many times people who go to Africa have this strong sense of identity with the land. They feel as if they're home, as if they've recently been in Africa. And by some design or chance of karma, this time they are a citizen in a different country.

But in their hearts, they're Africans. We also have Africans who feel they are at heart members of other countries.

In ECK, we have people from every country in the world. Other religions do too, but we are a new religion and many, many times smaller than Christianity, Islam, or the Hindu religion. Yet we have our members scattered over the entire world.

Driving in Nigeria

One of the members of ECK in Nigeria is named Mike. One day he said to the Inner Master in contemplation, "There are no other ECKist in this town. I wish there were others here."

Life is more difficult there; there are robberies right out in the street—even more than in the States. People's cars are stolen, they're forced out, sometimes harmed. They can lose their cars and everything else.

Mike got home one day and learned that his step-brother had just lost his car to some robbers.

They notified the police and did everything they could. The stepbrother was very upset. "The economy is so bad right now that this car was to last me for ten years," he said, "and now I have nothing."

Mike said, "But you have your life. You can always get another car, even if it takes ten years. You have your life. Who knows? If you had not had your car stolen you might have been driving down the street and been in an accident and lost your life that way."

If you've ever driven in Nigeria, you can understand this. Traffic is impressive here in Paris, but I think it's like riding on training wheels compared to Nigeria. Traffic there can take your breath away.

Africa is not the place to learn to drive an automobile. It is an experience. You're better off letting a citizen of Nigeria drive you around if you're there. It's better you don't try to do it yourself. It's not one of those do-it-yourself projects.

Back in the States we feel driving a car is pretty safe. But a couple of years ago the brakes went out on my car.

I had problems with the mechanics not doing a good job. American mechanics—Japanese car. Because the brakes failed, I ran into something. And for the last couple of years I've been healing from that accident.

Gratitude for Life

Mike's stepbrother's wife is a very devout born-again Christian. When she heard what Mike was saying she told her husband, "Your brother is speaking God's truth to us. We should be so grateful that you didn't lose your life.

"Many people lose their lives or are injured in car hijackings," the wife said. "He speaks the truth. Be thankful for your life."

So everybody felt better.

The next day a friend told the family that the stepbrother's car might have been found near another town. So Mike, his stepbrother, and two others went to identify the car.

On the way they stopped at a store. Another car drove up very quickly, some gunmen jumped out, and they started to hijack Mike's car.

Now Mike wasn't sure whether or not he was going to lose his life. So he began to sing the ancient name for God, HU. He sang HU to himself very quietly. One of the gunmen pointed to him and said, "Who's the driver of this car?" Mike said he was. "Get in the car," the man said,

"and start it." Mike said, "The car works; we drove here."
The robber said, "It's probably immobilized. Start it for
us."

So Mike started the car. Then he said, "You don't have
to hurt us. You have the car; you have all our possessions.
Just take it and go." And the robbers took Mike's car and
drove off with it.

It Never Hurts to Ask

The day before Mike had been preaching to his stepbrother how he should be thankful for his life. And now
he's sitting here by himself, with his own car stolen.

It was a very nice car too.

As soon as the gunman drove off, bystanders came
running up to offer their sympathy. But Mike said, "I'm
grateful for my life." Everyone was shocked; they couldn't
understand it. Somehow or another Mike and his stepbrother got home, filed the police report, and gave a
description of the car and the robbers.

Mike was happy, he was laughing. His family said,
"How can this be? How can you be so happy when they've
stolen your car?"

He said, "It's like I told my stepbrother yesterday: I
have my life."

Suddenly, he had to live his sermon. And he had to do
it with a true heart. But Mike turned it over to the Inner
Master, and he said, "Mahanta, don't let them have my
car unless it's necessary for my karma."

As the saying goes in ECK, it doesn't hurt to ask.

Mike wondered what would happen now. And the next
day, the police found the car. They read the license plate
number to him and he said, "Yes, this is my car." It had
been abandoned in a nearby town.

250

It turns out the car had had a mechanical defect, and it blew a piston. If you blow a piston in the engine the car is not going anywhere. So Mike got his car back. It never hurts to ask if you're in ECK.

The Golden Seed

Mike had a dream before this, and he asked the ECK Master Gopal Das, who used to serve centuries ago in Egypt, "Why are there no other people in my village who know about ECK or are members of ECK?"

Gopal Das had three golden seeds in his hand. He said to Mike, "Let's put these seeds in the soil."

As he planted them, he said, "The soil is ready. But the soil and the people need to be nurtured in just the right way, and the seed needs time to grow. Each seed will grow in its own time when it's ready."

Not long after the dream, Mike met the RESA, the ECK leader in Nigeria. The RESA said, "I know someone in your town who is an ECKist; I'll get his name to you so you can meet each other."

And so this connection happened, partly through the dream state and partly through a lot of other help, from inner guidance and inner protection. The ECK brought Mike protection from the robbers, plus guidance on where to find someone else in his town who is a member of ECK.

Fresh and Direct

The path of ECK is alive simply because it is of the Light and Sound of God. It is the freshest and most direct of the religions in the world today. Its destiny is to become a great spiritual teaching sometime.

By *great,* I don't mean that the teachings themselves

will become greater, because the teachings already are. But that the teachings will reach many, many people in many, many lands.

We in this generation will not see this growth, and our children will not see this destiny. But our grandchildren and their children will see it and benefit from the work that you are doing now, telling others about the Light and Sound of God.

I hope that in some way something that I've said to you will help you spiritually. Don't be surprised if you find people coming to you in your dreams who are willing to help you. But they will come only if you give them your permission to do so.

So, I would like to leave you with the golden seed. The golden seed is the message of ECK, the message of Divine Spirit in the world today in its freshest, most direct approach.

ECK European Seminar, Paris, France,
Saturday, July 31, 1993

What do you say when somebody coming to the teachings of ECK asks, "What's in it for me?"

14

Relaxed in the Arms of ECK

I appreciate that so many of you came to the ECK seminar here in Europe this year.

The economy is getting bad in some of your countries. In the United States we are supposedly coming out of our recession—or so we're told. And yet according to different polls on consumer spending and the like, people don't really believe it.

These are difficult times.

Advantages of the ECK Teachings

Last night I was mentioning some concerns about things on the political front, where different ethnic groups are going after each other after decades of control. Basically, this is the world we live in. And as I was thinking this over I said to myself, *I should make the advantages of the ECK teachings very clear.*

We can speak about the Light and Sound of God; we can speak about this being the most direct path to God and all that. But what do you say when somebody coming to the teachings of ECK asks, "What's in it for me?"

We're so used to talking about what we are that we

sometimes forget: maybe the people in ECK and those who are coming to ECK are looking for something.

Basically, what is the difference between ECKANKAR and the other religions?

The bottom line is simply this: The other religions—whether they know it or believe it—are dealing with the spiritual law of reincarnation.

Wheel of Reincarnation

In ECK we know that everybody is here because they've been here before. And they'll be here again. This is what we call this wheel of reincarnation or the wheel of karma. It just goes on for lifetime after lifetime after lifetime.

Christianity doesn't even teach reincarnation, but that doesn't mean that Christians are exempt from reincarnation.

People in the Christian faith believe that when you die, that's it. One life, one time, and after that heaven or hell. They don't know that they have come back before and they will come back again. They're on the Wheel of the Eighty-Four, which refers to the many thousands of lives that people live in the lower worlds through repeated lifetimes.

It gets to be old; it gets to be a very dreary cycle. And after a person has been here many times, there comes this feeling: Something's wrong with this scene, something's wrong with this script. Then people begin to wonder if there really is such a thing as only one lifetime.

They begin to look around.

Children Who Remember Past Lives

Today communication from all parts of the world is so good. Almost anytime you turn on the television, someone will be talking about reincarnation. And some of the stories are very, very good, such as those about children who remember past lives.

It's easy to discount such a story from an adult and say, "That's just another disillusioned person making up lies."

But it's harder when you have children coming up with past lifetimes, saying they have lived in another time and even describing certain settings and situations with a high degree of detail.

It's hard for people in a Christian society to accept this information. So they try to figure out another explanation for it, that it's some kind of mental transference. It would be a lot easier to just accept the fact of reincarnation.

But people in Christianity often can't. It would undermine their entire religion.

If they accepted reincarnation, for many it would mean the destruction of their faith. Because reincarnation is not a part of Christianity. But with all the information that's available today, more and more people are looking at the fact of rebirth. Some things suddenly make more sense within the context of reincarnation than outside of it. At that point a person will say, "I am looking for something beyond Christianity."

People on the Fringe

If someone is comfortable in Christianity, I make no attempt to pull them away. Because it would undermine their faith. But in every group—including ECK—there are always people on the fringe, those who are not quite sure of their religion. They're either coming into it, or they're on their way out.

This is true in every religion. There are always people

moving in and out of a teaching.

This is where you find the people who are looking and searching for truth. And this is where we have something to offer people. By the time they start looking for something else, they often have a suspicion that they have probably lived more lives than one.

The other people are learning what they need to know in Christianity. My feeling is, let them be. Leave them alone, and they'll come home—in time, when they're ready.

Living without Fear

Being relaxed in the arms of ECK presupposes living without fear.

But even when people first come to ECK—or even before they come to ECK—there is so much fear. There is so much fear.

One of the parts of ECKANKAR and the ECK teachings is Soul Travel. I don't talk about it as much as I used to, probably in deference to visitors who would come to the ECK seminars. They might feel that this is something very strange. But essentially Soul Travel is another way of saying "moving into a higher state of consciousness." And sometimes these experiences are very dramatic.

Soul Travel is a part of our teaching. I don't want to be so sensitive to the needs of new people that I forget to talk about our basic teachings. Soul Travel is but one of our teachings.

It Will Change Your Life

A young lady had driven her boyfriend to work one day. When she got back home, she decided to take a nap.

As she lay down, she suddenly felt this feeling of Soul

Travel. She's had several of these experiences before. Often it feels like somersaulting out of the body—like when you were young, playing with other kids, and you say, "OK, let's see if you can do a somersault." So you do a somersault on the floor, then the other child does a somersault. You try another one and knock the table over; then a parent comes in, and that's the end of somersaults in the house.

Sometimes you go out of the body this way. When I say out of the body, I mean in the sense that you are Soul in a body. You're not the body, this flesh cloth with so many fingers and so many arms, so many legs, usually one head. People get to thinking that this fleshly cloth is what they are, that this is their true identity.

It's not so. You are something else, inside this cloth of flesh.

Sometimes the ECK Masters will come to the people who are between paths, between one of the major religions and ECKANKAR. They'll come help the person out of the body.

Why would they do this? And what is the reaction of the person it's happening to?

When this happens, it will change your life. If you've not been a seeker before, after this experience of coming out of the body you will be. Why? Because suddenly you know more about the spiritual life than the teachers in your religion. Suddenly you know something you've never known before.

And now you begin to ask questions. This is usually the next step.

The Spiritual Clock

Many times a person who is taken out of the body by one of the ECK Masters was an ECK student in another

259

lifetime. The person may be born into a Christian family this life, for the experience—and to learn the basics of certain teachings that are very important to people. But the spiritual clock is ticking, and at a certain time this person is going to be ready to come to the path of ECK.

A few years before these inner changes are to begin, one of the ECK Masters may come to this person and give him a Soul Travel experience. At this point, the seeking begins in earnest. The person begins to ask questions of the teachers in his current religion.

If you're a newcomer, ask an ECKist, "How long have you been in ECK?" Then ask, "What happened to make you choose between the religion you were in before and ECKANKAR? What happened?" Sometimes it's a dramatic experience like Soul Travel. Sometimes it's something else, a feeling of divine love that the person felt with ECKANKAR.

But gradually there is movement away from the old teaching and toward the new teachings of ECK. Why?

Because Soul has heard the call of God and now wants to return home. It's that simple. And in Its desire to go home to God, to the true heavens, Soul will also leave the cycle of karma and reincarnation behind.

This is what we have to offer in ECK: how to get off the wheel of reincarnation.

Soul Travel Experience

When this young woman somersaulted out of the physical body, she became very frightened, even though she is an ECKist. She's had several Soul Travel experiences, because she is an adventuresome person. Not everyone has Soul Travel experiences. Some people simply do not go in for adventure of that kind. But this woman does.

Even so, when it happened, she was afraid. She said, "Oh, not now."

Why? Because she was afraid that she was dying. Suddenly she was not in the physical body anymore.

Most people think when you leave the physical body, that means death. It doesn't mean that at all. It actually means greater life and a fuller understanding of what's happening around you and who you are as a spiritual being.

It used to be that if you had an experience of being out of the body, you would have a very difficult time finding anyone who'd believe you. But in the last few years, with television shows and different books being written, everyone is pretty well getting used to the idea of out-of-the-body experiences. Many people have had them in one way or another. But it doesn't mean they know what the experience was all about. When they ask the orthodox minister or priest, these clergy often have no answer.

Scientists and therapists are still trying to figure out if it's some kind of mental aberration when people say they are out of the body. It's not a mental aberration. They are simply out of the body. The answer is sometimes simpler and makes more sense than some of the reasons that these people come up with.

Soul has—just for a short space of time—left the physical body and has come back.

Jump Start

There's nothing to fear in this. The ECK Masters approach someone who has been a member of ECK in a past lifetime but has forgotten because rebirth erases memories in many cases, at least by the age of six. The ECK Masters give the individual this experience, but they

261

stand by to see that no harm comes while this person is out of the body. After a few minutes, the person comes back in.

The person wakes up and tells everybody else in the family. Of course, the rest of the family are generally thinking, *Too bad, one of our own has become a mental case.* That's how it usually goes.

This is really funny, except if you happen to be the person.

Life becomes a very lonely walk from that moment on. You walk the earth, seeking answers to explain your experience. You find some answers here, some answers there, but it's all piecemeal. Each answer leads you on a little bit further; you get closer and closer. You're going through a real education.

The ECK Masters are there to jump-start you. But after that they leave you alone for five, ten, fifteen, or twenty years as you go from one path to another.

So many people who come to ECKANKAR began in one religion, then they had some kind of experience— either a very vivid dream or an experience out of the body through Soul Travel. They began to search in earnest for the answer as to what had happened to them. And they cover a lot of territory. They go through a lot of different paths—metaphysical groups, occult groups, different religions. They're always searching, always looking for the answer that rings true in their heart and can explain what happened to them so many years ago.

And then they come to the path of ECK.

Call of Soul

In ECK, we're very straightforward about karma and reincarnation—and for those who aren't timid—even Soul

Travel. For the timid, dream travel. These are the realities of those people who love God.

They love God more then anything else. And they have in the past. Their love for God in the past and in this lifetime is what qualifies them and you to approach the path of ECK.

Let's say you're new to ECK. You begin to ask around. You ask some of the initiates who've been in fifteen or twenty years, "What was it like? Why did you come to ECK?" You might be surprised to find that these Higher Initiates have nearly forgotten. They have almost forgotten the magic that occurred way back then. They have almost forgotten the lack of hope and the lack of love that was their life before something happened to them. And the despair, the loneliness, the despondency.

They have forgotten what it felt like to wonder, *What does this life mean?*

People in ECK today sometimes forget that life was once hell. It was torture. These people were willing to give up everything familiar, even the esteem of their families if necessary, to answer this call of Soul.

Searching for Answers

Why am I here? Where am I going? And when?

In the search for the answers to these questions, you learn the answers for life and death. You learn answers that even some of the most respected clergy of the major religions don't have a clue about.

By making this search yourself, after the ECK Masters get you started, you become more knowledgeable spiritually than your former teachers.

But even at that point, you find that you are at the foot of a new ladder.

What are these teachings? What do they involve? How will they change my life? How will they make me a better person? These are all questions you now must answer for yourself.

Test of Faith

When the young woman mentioned above somersaulted out of her body, she felt a pulling sensation, as often happens. She opened her eyes and found herself near the ceiling. Then she moved down the hallway, and she got scared.

"Please, I don't want to die now," she said. "I have a boyfriend, I'm happy. Let this experience stop."

So the experience stopped.

Not long after, she wrote me a letter apologizing. "I appreciate the experience," she told me, "and I want it again some other time, but not now."

So I said, "It's all right. Calm down, get yourself together. Take a couple more months, a couple more years; it doesn't make any difference. And if you're ever ready again, we'll show you something else which will amaze you. And if you're not too afraid, it will even delight you."

Fear is this thing that takes the joy out of living. It always does, every time it creeps in.

Even if you've been in ECK for many years, there are times your faith in ECK will be tested. There are times your hold on this physical life will be strained. Your faith in ECK will always come near the breaking point. Why?

To make you stronger spiritually.

The Weak Shall Never Have God

If you're going to become a Co-worker with God someday, you need to be strong. The weak shall never have God.

In the Christian Bible it says, "The meek shall inherit the earth." It's true, they shall inherit the earth. But who wants it? Even Christians are always talking about paradise, about leaving earth and getting to paradise. Yet they make a big thing about the meek inheriting the earth.

They never put two and two together. And when I dare to do it, people get upset with me for undermining their teachings.

I'm just pointing out the spiritual contradictions in a teaching.

They find comfort in the meek inheriting the earth because it means you're not going to leave the physical body and you're far from death. Paradise is what everyone says they aspire to. They say, "I want to go to heaven." But when the time comes, they're not ready to go. Why? Because it means giving up the physical body.

At this point people want to continue to be meek and inherit the earth.

It's this funny thing: They don't want to give up the earth and inherit heaven. I think they should try to inherit heaven.

I make these points, and later people begin to think about it. First they get upset. They feel, "This is wrong, this is all so wrong." After a couple of weeks they think, *I hate to say it, but it makes sense.*

The Man in the Light Blue Shirt

At the age of fifteen, a woman had a dream while she was living on her parents' farm. She dreamed she got up from her bed and walked down to the kitchen for a glass of water. As she was standing at the sink in her dream, looking out the window, she saw a blue spaceship land on a little hill.

Suddenly the woman felt something pulling her toward the spaceship. The next thing she knew, she was inside. She was flying through space, passing planets and galaxies. Then the spaceship turned around and rushed back to Earth faster than the speed of light. The woman saw all these things in the heavens that she had never seen before. The spaceship landed on the little knoll outside the kitchen window. She walked back to the house with a person wearing glasses and light blue shirt.

He said to her, "I'll come back for you when you're forty."

The woman woke up from this dream, thinking, *This is the most vivid dream I have ever had.*

Throughout her youth, this woman had said that she couldn't wait till she was forty. Now how many kids do you hear say that? And how many people in their thirties say they can't wait till they're forty? Somehow she knew that the age of forty, the decade of her forties, was going to be important for her. She didn't know why; she had forgotten that the spiritual traveler had told her that he'd come back for her when she was forty. All she remembered was that she couldn't wait till she was forty.

And so it happened. When she was forty, she introduced her sister to ECKANKAR.

A Gift for Another

You know how it is. People are always introducing other people to something else, buying gifts for other people that they themselves want. They make believe they don't, then buy it for someone else.

I get a lot of gifts like that. People give me something they really want for themselves. But they give it to me, and I don't want it. But you have to be polite and say, "Oh, gee. Just what I've always wanted." Then you wait awhile in case they come visit; you don't give it away too soon, you don't lose it too soon. A lot of times I just give it to someone who can use it or to some kind of charity.

My feeling is this: If I'm not going to use the gift, I would rather that someone else could. I know there's somebody out there who would want it.

This young woman knew that at the age of forty something important was going to happen. She was sort of interested in ECK, but instead of becoming a member of ECKANKAR herself, she told her sister about it.

So in the next two years her sister prepared this woman to become a member of ECKANKAR.

You know how this works. She finds the teachings of ECK, tells her sister, her sister becomes a member, then tells the one who told her about ECK how good the teachings are. Finally both sisters are members of ECKANKAR.

That Was the Master!

The woman had forgotten about the dream experience she'd had when she was fifteen, the experience with the spaceship.

One time during contemplation, after she became a member of ECKANKAR in her early forties, the woman suddenly remembered that dream. And she realized who the spiritual traveler was. The experience had taken place back in the 1960s.

During that time I was still wearing glasses.

I have contacts now, and when I'm not wearing the contacts, I wear glasses. And if I'm not wearing contacts or glasses, I'm just feeling my way around. This upsets some people. They say a spiritual master should have good eyesight.

I know a lot of people who have good eyesight, and they're not very far along spiritually.

Besides, if I really wanted to play the role—if it were so important to have perfect eyesight to be a master—I'd have one of those operations.

Whenever I do the simplest thing, even as simple as getting a new pair of glasses or contacts, it's difficult. It took me ten months last time with a very good optometrist. It took me five years before that with another very good optometrist. And I was never really satisfied. I go to people with the best credentials who have made all kinds of people happy. But when it comes to me, everything goes wrong.

So right now I'm not looking to have anyone practice surgery on me. Contacts are working just fine.

Healing Power of Writing

The theme for this seminar is "Sharing the Quest for Truth." And I've been talking about the different reasons people leave their paths and come to ECK.

There was an article in *Family Circle* magazine a few months ago. It talked about the healing power of writing about your problems.

In ECKANKAR we have initiate reports. A person becomes a Second Initiate after two years or so of study. I invite the person who has taken the Second Initiation to write a monthly initiate report.

This is to put down in writing the problems or concerns that you have in your daily life. And—remember this part—the spiritual benefits that have come to you since you've been a member of ECKANKAR. Or the spiritual experiences, such as Soul Travel, dream experiences, anything that gives you a better spiritual understanding of your life. This is what the initiate reports are for.

If you're a First Initiate who's had the dream initiation and you want to write a letter occasionally, please do. I read many of these physically. I read all of them the other way.

I get letters from people who are not members of ECK too. They write about some problem.

Family Circle magazine was commenting on a study of forty-one middle-aged professionals who had lost their jobs. Their careers were on the rocks. This study divided the forty-one people into three groups. The first group wrote about the trauma of having lost their job. And they did it for twenty minutes a day for five days straight. The second group wrote about a nontraumatic event for twenty minutes a day for five days. And the third group didn't write anything at all.

After eight months, the researchers looked at the group that had written about the pain and heartache and fear of losing their jobs. Half of these people were back at work.

Twenty-five percent of the group who wrote about anything, but not about the stress of losing their job, had found work. And in the third group—those people who didn't write anything at all—only 13.6 percent had found work.

The study was trying to show that people who write about their immediate problems are probably going to better be able to deal with those problems and get on with their lives.

Initiate Report Exercise

In ECK, you write the initiate report and you put down whatever is affecting you as well as the other things that

I mentioned—such as your dreams and experiences. You make a connection between your outer and your inner life. When you do this, I think you're going to find help. And it will be much more pronounced than what the people in the first group found, who simply wrote for five days for twenty minutes a day.

If you'll write an initiate report once a month, I think it'll help you very much.

It can be one or two pages. It doesn't have to be very long. Sometimes it can just be a few lines on a piece of paper. It's to help you.

When you write this letter, you're basically opening yourself up to the Inner Master and saying, "I've put my troubles down in front of me. I recognize these as problems, and I would like something to be done about them unless it's karma that is necessary to work off for my own spiritual unfoldment. Then I will accept that too." This is how you go about it.

A Question of Trust

One final thing: trusting the Inner Master. I don't put a lot of emphasis on trust with the Outer Master or even with the Inner Master. You have to be careful. If someone either on the inner or the outer tells you to do something that is against your code of ethics, it's wrong.

Out here, you can misunderstand something I'm saying. I will not knowingly mislead you. But there are teachers who will. So I don't put a lot of emphasis on trust and say, "Trust me."

Whenever I hear someone say, "Trust me," I immediately grab my wallet.

On the inner planes there are people who can put on the appearance of the Inner Master, of myself. They can do this. And if someone on the inside tells you to do something, such as harm someone or steal from someone, the person's wearing a mask. It is not the true Master. Don't act on any negative information, because it can't do you any good. And it can't do anyone else any good.

The true spiritual path is always working for the betterment of you and everyone around you.

When I say *your betterment,* I'm not talking about greed. I'm not saying convince that person to get into your business scam so that you can become rich. That won't do. That doesn't make it. You're going to find yourself tied more tightly than ever to the wheel of karma and reincarnation. I mention this because there are ECKists who prey on other ECKists, just as there are members of any religion who prey on members of their own religion.

There's a saying, "You can't cheat an honest man."

If people are cheated, sometimes it's because they were expecting to get something for nothing. And if you're expecting to get something for nothing and you've been cheated, next time check your own motives. And try to get your money back through the courts or whatever.

Twelve Red Roses

One Saturday afternoon a Higher Initiate was getting ready to officiate at an ECK Worship Service the next day. She wasn't expecting many people to attend, but she'd been thinking she'd like to bring two things to the ECK Worship Service. One would be a picture of the spiritual leader of ECK, and the other would be a small bouquet of flowers. She thought this would be a nice balance.

As she was preparing what she would say at the worship service, she realized she had forgotten to get flowers. It was a hot summer day.

271

"Oh, well," she said, "at least we'll have the picture. We can have the flowers some other time."

She went into contemplation and began an inner conversation with the Inner Master. She was doing this within herself, a mental conversation. Sometimes when people do this they're not sure if they're just talking to themselves or if they're actually talking to the Inner Master. Other people have this conversation very clearly; they know without a doubt.

She and the Inner Master talked about this and that, and she was enjoying the conversation. Suddenly the Inner Master said, "You need to get those flowers."

"It's a hot day," she said, "and traffic is very bad in the afternoon between my home and the store." "You need the flowers for tomorrow," he said.

So she said, "OK, I'll get the flowers."

It was late in the day, and she figured the flower shop wouldn't have any flowers. But why not try?

The owner of the flower store was a very pleasant, elderly woman. They looked at the flowers outside, but they weren't the right kind. The Higher Initiate was thinking they really should be a dozen roses. So she said to the owner, "I'd like twelve roses."

"We have some in here," the woman said.

She showed the Higher Initiate twelve roses lying in the refrigerated case.

"I can put these in a box with some greens and ribbon," the owner said. But the ECK initiate was thinking, *That means I'm going to have to go home, cut the stems, find a vase, and arrange the flowers.* She didn't want to bother with all that.

So she looked a little further, and way back up on the top shelf of the refrigerated case, she saw twelve roses in a vase all ready to go. So she bought them, put them in her car, and began driving home.

As she drove, she began another conversation with the Inner Master, thinking to herself, *After the worship service tomorrow these roses will look very pretty in my home.* But then she said to the Inner Master, "I give these roses to you out of gratefulness and thanks for all the love you have given me, for the companionship and the friendship, because no matter where I am you are always there."

And the Master said, "All right then, since you gave the roses to me, tomorrow give one to each person who comes to the ECK Worship Service."

How beautiful these roses would have been in my home after the service! the woman thought. So she said to the Master, "But there probably won't be enough roses to go around." He answered, "Just take the roses." "Well, what do I do? Tell people when the service is over that I'll give each one a rose until they run out?"

"Just take the roses," the Master said. "Give one to each person."

She said, "Really?" And he said, "Trust me." So she said, "OK. How much can you lose with a dozen roses?"

Eleven people came to the worship service the next day. There was a rose for each one of them. The Higher Initiate wrote me this story, and at the bottom of her letter she said, "Thank you for the rose."

She didn't get a dozen, but one rose can be a very special gift of love.

Relaxed in the Arms of ECK

Relaxed in the arms of ECK means giving up and letting go of your fear. Giving up and letting go of your

273

fear to Divine Spirit. Because that is the ECK, the Holy Spirit.

These seminars are like family gatherings, where we come together. And I can assure you that you will be blessed many times over for having taken the trouble to come. The blessings will be returned to you many times, over and over again, when you return home.

I would like to wish you a safe journey home—both you and your loved ones as you travel home here. And I'll be with you on your journey home to God. May the blessings be.

ECK European Seminar, Paris, France,
Sunday, August 1, 1993

Glossary

Words set in SMALL CAPS are defined elsewhere in this glossary.

ARAHATA. An experienced and qualified teacher for ECKANKAR classes.

CHELA. A spiritual student.

ECK. The Life Force, the Holy Spirit, or Audible Life Current which sustains all life.

ECKANKAR. Religion of the Light and Sound of God. Also known as the Ancient Science of SOUL TRAVEL. A truly spiritual religion for the individual in modern times, known as the secret path to God via dreams and SOUL TRAVEL. The teachings provide a framework for anyone to explore their own spiritual experiences. Established by Paul Twitchell, the modern-day founder, in 1965.

ECK MASTERS. Spiritual Masters who can assist and protect people in their spiritual studies and travels. The ECK Masters are from a long line of God-Realized SOULS who know the responsibility that goes with spiritual freedom.

HU. The most ancient, secret name for God. The singing of the word HU, pronounced like the word *hue,* is considered a love song to God. It is sung in the ECK Worship Service.

INITIATION. Earned by the ECK member through spiritual unfoldment and service to God. The initiation is a private ceremony in which the individual is linked to the Sound and Light of God.

LIVING ECK MASTER. The title of the spiritual leader of ECKANKAR. His duty is to lead SOULS back to God. The Living ECK Master can assist spiritual students physically as the Outer Master, in the dream state as the Dream Master, and in the spiritual worlds as the

275

Inner Master. Sri Harold Klemp became the MAHANTA, the Living ECK Master in 1981.

MAHANTA. A title to describe the highest state of God Consciousness on earth, often embodied in the LIVING ECK MASTER. He is the Living Word.

PLANES. The levels of heaven, such as the Astral, Causal, Mental, Etheric, and Soul planes.

SATSANG. A class in which students of ECK study a monthly lesson from ECKANKAR.

THE SHARIYAT-KI-SUGMAD. The sacred scriptures of ECKANKAR. The scriptures are comprised of twelve volumes in the spiritual worlds. The first two were transcribed from the inner PLANES by Paul Twitchell, modern-day founder of ECKANKAR.

SOUL. The True Self. The inner, most sacred part of each person. Soul exists before birth and lives on after the death of the physical body. As a spark of God, Soul can see, know, and perceive all things. It is the creative center of Its own world.

SOUL TRAVEL. The expansion of consciousness. The ability of SOUL to transcend the physical body and travel into the spiritual worlds of God. Soul Travel is taught only by the LIVING ECK MASTER. It helps people unfold spiritually and can provide proof of the existence of God and life after death.

SOUND AND LIGHT OF ECK. The Holy Spirit. The two aspects through which God appears in the lower worlds. People can experience them by looking and listening within themselves and through SOUL TRAVEL.

SPIRITUAL EXERCISES OF ECK. The daily practice of certain techniques to get us in touch with the Light and Sound of God.

SUGMAD. A sacred name for God. SUGMAD is neither masculine nor feminine; IT is the source of all life.

WAH Z. The spiritual name of Sri Harold Klemp. It means the Secret Doctrine. It is his name in the spiritual worlds.

Index

Abortion, 127
Accounting story, 224
Acorns, 31–33
Acting (actions), 16, 128, 180, 205, 207
Acupuncturist, 144
Adjustments, 56. *See also* Change (changing)
Adler, Alfred, 216
Affront, taking, 13
Africa, 61, 247–48, 249
Agent, divine, 208
Airplane story, 99–101
Air travel, 199
Alaska, 155–56
American dream, 138, 190
Angel(s), 85, 103, 153, 189
Anger (angry)
  filled with, 179
  getting, 98, 186
  letting go of, 35–36, 76, 188
  with others, 79
  people, 142
  working out, 235
Animals, 144, 179. *See also* Ant; Bird(s); Blackbirds; Blue jays; Cardinals; Cat; Chipmunks; Deer; Dog; Dolphins; Family (families): of animals; Goldfinch; Rabbit; Raccoons; Sparrows; Squirrels; Turkey; Turtle-doves

Answers, searching for, 262, 263. *See also* Question(s)
Ant, 48, 175–76
Appreciation, 33. *See also* Gratitude
Argument, 96
Asking, 115–16, 250–51
Attention, 21, 209. *See also* God: focus on
Attitude, 79, 102
Australia, 71
Authority, 185
Awareness. *See also* Consciousness
  expanding in, 50
  through gratitude, 36
  greater, 155, 178, 208
  lack of, 46, 75
  levels of, 43, 178, 179, 180
  of the Light of God, 131
  of ourselves as Soul, 50
  of the purpose of this existence, 109
  spiritual, 61, 179, 197

Balance, 53
Bank robbery, 33–34
Baseball-shoes story, 180–81, 184–85
Behavior, 152, 153, 179, 180. *See also* Acting (actions)
Being(s), spiritual
  becoming a more, 102, 109,

277

278

relaxed in the arms of, 258,
273
telling others about, 68, 208,
233
ECKANKAR
books, 35, 87, 155, 241. *See
also Flute of God, The;
Shariyat-Ki-Sugmad, The;
Stranger by the River;
Tiger's Fang, The; Unlocking the Puzzle Box,* Mahanta
Transcripts, Book 6
coming to, 39–40, 41, 50, 201,
256, 258, 260, 263, 266–67,
268
difference between, and other
religions, 256
discourses, 5, 241
dream discourses, 9
early days of, 145
elements of path of, 177–78
essential precept in, 102
and female ECK Masters. *See*
ECK Masters: male and
female
finding, 64–65, 169
first coming into, 235–36
future of, 133, 205
helping others find, 50, 236
hurting, 227
individual in, 139
introductory talks on, 156
is an individual path, 42
leadership of, 247
life in, 39, 42, 48, 188–89
meeting others in, 197–99
member(s) of, 10, 61, 65, 123,
142, 201, 202, 204, 235, 240,
247, 251, 267
members of, in a past life, 239,
259, 261
message of, 131, 191, 252
new member of, 5
no hurry in, 64
open house, 227–28
organization of, 207

people who come to, 90, 207,
248, 262, 263
purpose of, 139–40
our purpose in, 207
as Religion of the Light and
Sound of God, 241
seminars. *See* Seminar(s),
ECKANKAR
size of, 248
teachings. *See* Teaching(s)
writings, 5, 106
ECKANKAR Journal, 67–68
ECKANKAR Spiritual Center,
13, 241
ECK center, 238–39
ECKist(s)
experience of, 62–63, 64
and healing professions, 25
life of, 37
and love, 78, 198
nature of, 43
our goal as, 134
ECK Master(s), 153. *See also*
Dream Master; Fubbi
Quantz; Gopal Das; Inner
Master; Living ECK Master;
Mahanta; Master(s)(ship);
Peddar Zaskq; Rebazar
Tarzs; Twitchell, Paul
and their expectations of
chelas, 205
get you started on the spiritual path, 262, 263
help find the seeker, 236, 238
help from, 170, 239–40, 241,
259–60, 261–62
male and female, 19, 20, 28, 34
meeting, 22–23
mission of, 170
teach us, 63, 64
ECK-Vidya, 42, 178
ECK Worship Service, 223, 229,
271–73
Ecology, 57–59
Economy (economist), 136–37,
189, 255

281

Hardship(s), 85, 208, 221, 246, 247
Harmony, 76, 234
Hate (hatred), 179, 235
Healing(s). *See also* Chiropractor; Dentist; Doctor(s); Holy Spirit: healing from; Optometrist; Psychotherapy
  as aspect of ECK teachings, 178
  different areas of, 45
  from God, 47, 118
  through HU, 212
  through love, 124
  methods of, 47, 144
  through past-life therapy, 25–26
Health, 154, 246
Hearing, inner, 212
Heart
  answers in, 35, 262
  awakened, 115, 118, 123
  heaven within, 140
  when love enters the, 121
  love, wisdom, and freedom within, 233
  open(ing), 5–6, 7, 45, 123, 178, 179–80, 194, 207, 208
  secrets of, 67
  true, 250
Heartbreak, 208
Heaven(s). *See also* Plane(s); World(s)
  concept of, in ECKANKAR, 102
  desire for, 244, 260
  first step toward, 84
  going to, 122
  levels of, 11, 77, 169
  never be a, on earth, 133, 140
  nobody can carry us to, 191
  Soul lived in, 83
  as state of consciousness, 57
  within your heart, 140
Hell, 57, 244
Help, 42, 43, 50, 166, 228, 229.

See also Dream Master: help from; Dream(s)(ing): help through; ECK Master(s): help from; Holy Spirit: help from; HU: help through; Spirit, Divine: help from; Twitchell, Paul: help from
Herbs, 144
Hernia-operation story, 192–93
Higher Initiate(s), 200–201, 263, 271–73
History, 179
Holy Spirit. *See also* ECK; Spirit, Divine
  becoming one with, 242
  cues from, 218
  feeds the lower worlds, 86
  God created through, 235
  healing from, 45, 47
  help from, 140
  insight from, 37, 188
  Light and Sound of God as, 78, 86, 91, 242
  nature of, 78
  open to, 50, 75, 91, 226
  principles of, 77
  servant for, 223
  speaks to us, 61, 175, 193
  as Voice of God, 91, 193
  works on your behalf, 61
  works with us, 37, 42
Home, 83–84, 237
Hope, 263
HU. *See also* Spiritual Exercises of ECK
  allows Light of God to enter, 62–63
  attention on, 209
  as a first step toward truth, 84
  healing through, 212
  help through, 7–8
  Mahanta gives the, 77, 91, 108
  as name for God, 8, 123–24
  nature of, 108, 188
  opens the heart, 123, 194, 207

as precious gem, 108–9
protection through, 39
to raise consciousness, 48, 76,
    160–61
sound of, 87–88
as spiritual exercise, 6, 37, 75,
    108, 222
telling others about, 7,
    8, 9, 140, 160, 188,
    193, 194, 208
when in trouble, 77, 140, 141,
    211–12, 229, 250
when you're worried, 192–93
with your whole heart, 148
Human(s). *See also* Love:
    human; Relationships:
    human; Wisdom: human
    being(s), 4, 131, 132, 179, 242,
        244
    condition, 139
    faculties can't define God, 79
    family, 143
    form, 127, 178
    imperfect, 128
    nature, 72, 80, 82, 144, 205,
        238, 240
    plane, 92
    race, 14, 24
    terms, 78
Humble, 158, 223, 227
Hurricane Andrew, 145
Hypnosis (hypnotism), 25, 26, 46

Icebergs, fear of, 243
Ice cream, 182–84, 202
Illness, 105
Images, 152, 153
Imagination, 9, 151
Impatience, 107
Independence, spiritual, 190
Inflation, 225
Initiate report, 268–69, 270
Initiate(s). *See also* ECKist(s);
    Higher Initiate(s)
    ECK, 35, 186, 238

First, 269
Second, 64, 268
Initiation(s), 205
    dream, 236, 269
    First, 236
    Fourth, 200
    Second, 200, 268
    Third, 200
    wanting the next, 64, 206
Injustice, 191
Inner and outer. *See* Connection,
    between inner and outer life
Inner Master. *See also* Dream
    Master; Living ECK Master;
    Mahanta; Outer Master
    attention on, 209
    chooses your family, 245
    communication with, 157, 158,
        159, 164, 248, 272, 273
    connection with, 247
    as Dream Master, 38
    experience with, 228, 243–44
    and First Initiation, 236
    friendship with, 273
    as fundamental in ECK, 35
    guidance from, 44
    how the, works, 45, 207, 210–12
    as the Mahanta, 223
    message from, 36
    nature of, 222
    opening to, 270
    presence of, 213
    relationship with, 202
    surrendering to, 250
    trusting the, 154, 270–71
Inquisition, 134
Insight(s), 7, 42, 198
Intelligence, 4
Intuition, 155, 157
Islam, 134, 236. *See also*
    Muslim(s)

Jade master, the, 106–8
Job(s)
    attitude toward our, 55–57,
        101–2

to others, 128, 139
self-, 28, 29, 120, 168
Restaurant, 73–74
Retirement, 37
Revenge, 126
Right(s), 14, 185, 193
Roman Catholic Church. *See*
    Catholic(ism); Catholic-man
    story
Roman Empire, 21–22, 140
Roses, 271–73
Rules, 76, 77, 106
Russia, 139. *See also* Soviet
    Union

Saint Paul, 11, 168, 169
Saints, 21, 22
Salary cap, 137–38
School system, 146
Scientists, 73
Scriptures, 194. *See also*
    Bible(s); *Shariyat-Ki-*
    Sugmad, The
Search(ing), 238, 262, 263
Seat-at-the-seminar story, 176–
    77
Security-guard story, 62
Seeing, 61, 76
Seeker, 259
Self(-). *See also* Discipline: self-;
    Responsibility (responsibili-
    ties): self-; Self-Realization
    direction, 128
    image, 46
    little, 177
    petty, 144
    righteousness, 27, 28
    sufficient, 147, 191–92
Selfishness, 177, 200, 235, 245
Self-Realization, 200
Seminar(s), ECK(ANKAR), 13,
    170
    after, 209–10
    coming to, 109, 255
    ECK African, 247
    experience at, 122–23

facing fears at, 210
like family gatherings, 274
love at, 209
meeting others at, 199
1993 ECK Springtime, 176
1992 ECK South Pacific
    Regional, 167
people around you benefit
    from, 109
shake-up before an, 209
talks at, 141, 258
theme, 268
Seriously, taking ourselves too,
    14
Serve (serving) (service), 23, 50,
    83, 103, 134, 220
Shakespeare, 199
Shariyat-Ki-Sugmad, The, 5, 50
Sign, 61
Sin(s), 60, 125, 128
Skeptics, 73, 90
Slaves, 190
Smoking, 165–66
Socialism, 133, 135–39, 141,
    147–48
Society, 59
Socrates, 199
Somalia, 152–53
Soul(s)
    awareness of, 50, 178
    becoming godlike, 15
    body, 168
    in a body, 49, 259
    call of, 263
    and creation, 178, 179
    doorway to aspects of, 178
    on earth, 139
    exists because God loves It,
        118, 127, 161
    fear separates, from God's
        love, 210
    God's love for, 175
    has lived in many countries,
        247
    hears the call of God, 16, 260
    is eternal, 49, 127, 161, 227

How to Take the Next Step on Your Spiritual Journey

Find your own answers to questions about your past, present, and future through the ancient wisdom of ECKANKAR. Take the next bold step on your spiritual journey.

ECKANKAR can show you why special attention from God is neither random nor only for a few saints. It is for anyone who opens his heart to Divine Spirit, the Light and Sound of God.

Are you looking for the secrets of life and the afterlife? Sri Harold Klemp, today's spiritual leader of ECKANKAR, and Paul Twitchell, its modern-day founder, have written a series of monthly discourses that give unique Spiritual Exercises of ECK. They can lead you in a direct way to God. Those who join ECKANKAR, Religion of the Light and Sound of God, can receive these monthly discourses.

As a Member of ECKANKAR You'll Discover

1. The most direct route home to God through the ECK teachings of the Light and Sound. Plus the opportunity to gain wisdom, charity, and spiritual freedom in this lifetime through the ECK initiations.
2. The spiritual meaning of dreams, Soul Travel techniques, and ways to establish a personal relationship with Divine Spirit through study of monthly discourses. These discourses are for the entire family. You may study them alone at home or in a class with others.
3. Secrets of self-mastery in a Wisdom Note and articles by the Living ECK Master in the *Mystic World,* a quarterly newsletter. In it are also letters and articles from ECK members around the world.
4. Upcoming ECK seminars and other activities worldwide, new study materials from ECKANKAR, and more, in special mailings. Join the excitement. Have the fulfilling experience of attending major ECK seminars!
5. The joy of the ECK Satsang (discourse study) experience in classes and book discussions. Share spiritual experiences and find answers to your questions about the ECK teachings.

How to Find Out More

To request membership in ECKANKAR using your credit card (or for a free booklet on membership) call (612) 544-0066, weekdays, between 8:00 a.m. and 5:00 p.m., central time. Or write to: ECKANKAR, Att: Information, P.O. Box 27300, Minneapolis, MN 55427 U.S.A.

Introductory Books on ECKANKAR

What Is Spiritual Freedom?
Mahanta Transcripts, Book 11
Harold Klemp

Discover your full power as a spiritual being. Through stories and twenty-three techniques, Harold Klemp shows how to get to the spiritual root of your problems and take your next step on the road to spiritual freedom.

ECKANKAR—Ancient Wisdom for Today

Are you one of the millions who have heard God speak through a profound spiritual experience? This introductory book will show you how dreams, Soul Travel, and experiences with past lives are ways God speaks to you. An entertaining, easy-to-read approach to ECKANKAR. Reading this little book can give you new perspectives on your spiritual life.

Stories to Help You See God in Your Life
The Book of ECK Parables, Volume 4
Harold Klemp

Harold Klemp masterfully weaves parable after parable out of the most humble of circumstances. He shows us how to look for God in the little things. In this book you'll discover how to listen to God, better understand your dreams and your relationships with others, and recognize the miracles in your life.

HU: A Love Song to God
(Audiocassette)

Learn how to sing an ancient name for God, HU (pronounced like the word *hue*). A wonderful introduction to ECKANKAR, this two-tape set is designed to help listeners of any religious or philosophical background benefit from the gifts of the Holy Spirit. It includes an explanation of the HU, stories about how Divine Spirit works in daily life, and exercises to uplift you spiritually.

For fastest service, phone (612) 544-0066 weekdays between 8 a.m. and 5 p.m., central time, to request books using your credit card, or look under **ECKANKAR** in your phone book for an ECKANKAR center near you. Or write: **ECKANKAR, Att: Information, P.O. Box 27300, Minneapolis, MN 55427 U.S.A.**

There May Be an
ECKANKAR Study Group near You

ECKANKAR offers a variety of local and international activities for the spiritual seeker. With hundreds of study groups worldwide, ECKANKAR is near you! Many areas have ECKANKAR Centers where you can browse through the books in a quiet, unpressured environment, talk with others who share an interest in this ancient teaching, and attend beginning discussion classes on how to gain the attributes of Soul: wisdom, power, love, and freedom.

Around the world, ECKANKAR study groups offer special one-day or weekend seminars on the basic teachings of ECKANKAR. Check your phone book under **ECKANKAR**, ☎ or call **(612) 544-0066** for membership information and the location of the ECKANKAR Center or study group nearest you. Or write **ECKANKAR, Att: Information, P.O. Box 27300, Minneapolis, MN 55427 U.S.A.**

☐ Please send me information on the nearest ECKANKAR Center or study group in my area.

☐ Please send me more information about membership in ECKANKAR, which includes a twelve-month spiritual study.

Please type or print clearly   839

Name _____
　　　　　　first (given)　　　　　　　　　　last (family)

Street_____ Apt. # _____

City _____ State/Prov. _____

ZIP/Postal Code _____ Country _____

Eva K. Bowlby Public Library
311 North West Street
Waynesburg, PA 15370